Homegrown Music

Homegrown Music

By MARC BRISTOL

MADRONA PUBLISHERS
SEATTLE

Published by
Madrona Publishers, Inc.
2116 Western Avenue
Seattle, Washington 98121

First Edition
10 9 8 7 6 5 4 3 2 1

Library of Congress Cataloging in Publication Data

Bristol, Marc, 1949-
Homegrown music.

Bibliography: p.

1. Music trade. 2. Music, Popular (Songs, etc.) — Instruction and study. 3. Folk music — Instruction and study. 4. Musical instruments — Construction. I. Title.
ML3790.B74 1982 780 82-17217
ISBN 0-914842-91-9

Portions of this book have appeared previously in *The Mother Earth News* in somewhat different form.

PHOTO CREDITS

Brent Thorgren: frontispiece and pages 7, 12, 73; Richard Tubbs, pages 4, 8, 9, 63, 64, 65, 71, 85, 88, 89; Marc Bristol, pages 15, 17, 23, 29, 32, 34, 38, 40, 69, 80, 92, 129; Vicki Bolom, page 14; Tom Allen, page 19; G.L. Rodgers, page 77; Linda Lengacher, page 84. The photo on page 5 is courtesy of Clarence Bristol.

To my grandmother,
Winona Erickson,
for leading me to the country
where I found my music

Acknowledgments

Much of the material in this book has appeared previously in different form as part of my column, "Homegrown Music," in *The Mother Earth News*. I've drawn from four years of columns to build this book, and since the column is an ongoing affair, presumably we'll put together a second volumn after another couple of years or so. This book owes a great debt to the editors of *The Mother Earth News*, both for having maintained the column as a regular feature and for their editorial skills, which have influenced the expression of my ideas.

There are a great many other people to thank, more than I am able to list here, so what follows is only a partial list. Many people, including readers of the column who've written to me, have provided me with information that I've used in writing my column, as well as this book.

The best place to start the list is with Richard Tubbs, who not only contributed several photos to illustrate the book, but printed *my* photos, too. None of the photos here have appeared in the column, though Richard submitted a batch quite some time ago at my request. It's really been wonderful having someone take such a strong interest in the project, particularly a multitalented person like Richard.

I feel that space may limit my ability to express my gratitude, so here comes the limited expression: Thanks to Gary Cools, for turning me on to the Jim Kweskin Jug Band; to Billy Hults for keeping washboard music alive through some lean years; to Quentin Rhoton for maintaining the bass line; to my aunt, Betty Austin, for encouraging me to be different; to Dan Wallace for the professional musical saw; and to all of the following for their various contributions to the content of this book:

Ann Adams
Vicki Bolom
William Boothe
Bruce Bratton
Faith Conlon
David Cross
Jimmie Fadden
Mark Filler

Dennis Flanagan
Emily Friedman and the *Come For To Sing* staff
Jeff Hanna
Bill Hires
Dale Hustler
Bruce Kaplan
Dan Kersten
Rich Kuras
Patrick Leonard
Anschway Livingproof
Chris Lunn
Jim McLaughlin
Tim Olsen
Todd Parks
Kevin Potter
Tom Scribner
Irene Scyriver
John Sebastian
Phyl Sheridan
Jeffrey D. Smith
Jerry Snyder
Mike Tagawa
Mark Talaba
Thomas Thomas
Larry Van Over
Phil and Vivian Williams
Wyatt Wood

Recorded versions of the songs included in this book are available through King Noodle Records, Box 25, Duvall, Washington 98019. Thanks here to Steve Babcock for making that part of the project possible.

Preface: The Expanding Universe of Music

No one knows exactly how or when people first started using music as a part of their daily lives and rituals. It's easy to visualize a group of primitive people celebrating after a big feast, when the bellies are full and everyone is happy. Someone discovers that a hollow bone or log makes a nice noise, and begins to do it rhythmically. Soon someone else comes up with another sound and uses it to make a variation on the rhythm. Eventually everyone joins in making some sort of sound in time to the original rhythm.

The jam session then becomes synonymous with the good times, and people begin to use music in attempt to bring back those good times, whether in a hunting ritual, a mating dance, or whatever. The fact that these occasions are the highlights of life encourages experimentation for new sounds, either to add to the fun or to obtain some recognition at the next celebration. It's fun to imagine how each type of instrument was originally discovered or invented—one can picture things such as a hide, stretched on a rack for curing, falling on top of a large bowl and creating the first drum.

Some of the instruments I discuss in this book are actually not-too-distant relatives of primitive musical instruments. The washboard, for example, descended from a scraper made from an animal's jawbone. The washtub bass comes from an African instrument called the ground bow, which was a hide stretched over a pit in the ground. The center of the hide was connected by means of a gut string to a small sapling bent over the hole. Messages were sent through miles of jungle using these ground bows, which were originally developed from a type of animal trap. Possibly they were used to invite the neighboring villages to feasts and get-down jam sessions!

My point is that without experimentation we wouldn't have music, certainly not in the forms it takes today. I give a lot of suggestions for getting started in music and ways to proceed once you have embarked on that course of self-expression. But I want you to realize that you shouldn't necessarily be trying to do this in a way that has been done before—particularly if you've been frustrated trying to imitate a sound you've heard. Express *yourself*! You are a unique individual and *your* sound may not be like anyone else's.

As in everything, of course, there has to be a balance. So when you're playing music with others (or even for others), rhythm and harmony are important factors. You make your own unique sound in time with the rhythm and in harmony with unique sounds of other individuals. It's this very nature of music that enables an individual to exist within, and feel connected to, a larger cultural framework.

Individualism has always been a primary theme of American culture. And one reason I feel American music has become so popular throughout the world is the fact that it has been an experimental mix of various cultural and ethnic influences. For example, what we call our "country music" has been cross-bred from Northern European folk music, African melodic and rhythmic themes, and a wide variety of other traditional sources. In fact, whenever some bright individual blends two formerly independent cultural sounds it tends to become a new, ear-catching form of music.

The people of all countries yearn to realize their oneness—and our American melting-pot music helps to point the way. We *can* live together in harmony, and the music proves it. Music is a universal language.

If you haven't yet started to play music, I hope you can find encouragement here for taking the first step, as well as some useful information to help you know what the next step might be. If you've already embarked on your musical journey, I still think you'll find some inspiration and information in this book. Anyone who plays knows that the overall level of music appreciation is always higher if more people participate, and there are plenty of suggestions here for helping others get into it and enjoy the fun.

Contents

1: Finding Your Own Music 3

2: Making Your Own Instruments 9

3: Acquiring and Recycling Used Instruments 31

4: Learning to Play the Guitar 42

5: Jamming and Song-Swapping 60

6: Making Money with Homegrown Music 68

7: Doing Your Own Recording at Home 75

8: Writing Your Own Tunes 82

9: Attending Folk Music Festivals 87

Song Section 93

Resources 112

- Mail-Order Houses 112
- Folk Music Publications 117
- Homegrown Music on Records 121
- Construction and Repair Manuals, and Other Books 124

Homegrown Music

1

Finding Your Own Music

LET'S say you're one of those people who've been heard to say, "Gosh I wish I could play a musical instrument!" Those of us who do play hear that quite a bit. Maybe you've never come out and said it, but you were thinking it every time you came across someone pickin' and grinnin' or some group having a great time jamming out on a happy tune. If so, this book is for you — whether you've already taken some of the first steps, or whether you always finish the wish by saying, "But all I can play is the radio." If you like music well enough to *want* to play, you *can*.

We all have rhythm in the beat of our hearts, and rhythm is the basis of music. Even harmony is basically rhythm, as I'll explain later in this chapter. So the first thing you need to do is just to stop telling yourself you can't play music. Telling yourself you can't is the only reason you can't. Once you stop saying that, you're ready for step two, which is getting started.

First thing, you'll have to pick an instrument. Now that choice needn't be a hard one to make. For one thing, you were born with several choices built in. I mean you can clap your hands! You can snap your fingers! You can whistle and sing! Or you can dance while doing all of these things! That's right — dancing is a way of making music. Speaking as a professional musician, I can say that when someone puts his entire body into the music you're playing, it can be just like a jump start for a dead hot rod. I advocate ecstasy!

So next time you hear some folks playing music — join in somehow.

If you really enjoy music, you can see the logic in the idea that the closer you are to it, the greater the pleasure. You want to feel that music moving *through* you. Even if you own a musical instrument, there are going to be times when you're with people who are playing music and you don't have your instrument with you. And there are going to be plenty of times when you're by yourself, feeling music, with no other instruments than your hands, your voice, and your whole body. Let the music take you. Give yourself to it!

Even if you decide you've just got to become a guitar player, a banjo picker, or piano plunker, there may be a period of waiting before you get your hands on a decent instrument. Any time you put in between now and then getting right into music with some part

Shade Tree jam session at the Northwest Regional Folklife Festival.

(or all) of your body is going to help you become a musician.

Actually, there are several wonderful styles of music that traditionally feature only the human voice, or the voice with hand-clapping. A capella singing (with no instrument accompaniment), which has always been an important form of human expression, is now enjoying a resurgence of popularity. In fact, this one very simple and low-cost method of making music—if thoroughly explored—can keep you occupied all by itself for a long, long time. There are choirs you could join, for instance, plus barbershop quartets and choruses. You could try your vocal chords on Philadelphia street-style "doo-wop," field hollers, and shape-note singing, which is an Appalachian gospel style. There's also mantra singing as done by Buddhists and others before meals and at celebrations. There are Native American chants and Polynesian chants and sea chanteys and—well, you get the idea.

It's so easy to slip into music this way. Just open your mouth and sing. Don't worry about how you sound at first. Even little birds have to practice before they can sing—or fly, for that matter! You'll be soaring soon enough yourself, if you'll just practice a lot, anywhere and anytime you get the chance. I received my own voice training while delivering pizzas in my car and singing along with the radio. In music the word *practice* doesn't have to mean something you do in preparation for performance. It *is* performance, like the practice of medicine. It's something you do every day, the way you respond to life.

It's natural that some of you will be shy about singing in the company of others at first. So sing by yourself, and sing as loud as you can. On most instruments you have to wail for a while full tilt before you can get enough control for subtler expression. It's great fun to wail, too! You'll develop your self-confidence through learning what you can do with your voice. The music you make can help you find out who you are. Music is soul-to-body communication when you really let yourself go and get deep into it.

A barbershop quartet (author's father is second from left).

There's no need to try to push your public debut before you're ready for it. First and foremost, your music must please *you*. I've spent many enjoyable hours playing and singing just for myself out on the front porch or out in a field. Often when I'm doing this, I'll suddenly flash that I have an audience—it's the dandelions or, really, all the plants and birds—all creation. When you communicate with *yourself*, in the process you'll connect with the oneness of all things.

Humans are basically social and gregarious, though—even the shy ones. Everyone, whether or not he or she will admit it, wants to reach out and communicate with others. And one of the easiest and most satisfying ways to do that reaching out is with your voice—musically.

If you exercise your singing voice until you're comfortable with it, sooner or later you will find yourself with people who make you feel that you can express yourself musically with them, and they will approve. Once you get past that hurdle, the race is as good as won. That's when the real magic will begin. Every time you sing your very best for others after that, it will be better than your last best effort.

The same principles apply to getting your start playing a "real" musical instrument. Your voice, your hands, and your body are yours naturally, and if you wish to take up some other instrument, you'll need to get one that's your own before you can really learn to play it. Sure, you can learn chords and plunk on someone else's guitar. But music is a magical connection, and the instrument has to become part of you before you can speak through it or sing through it. It needs to live with you for a while.

There are many ways to acquire musical instruments, some of which will be discussed in following chapters. Some you can make yourself. Some are store-bought, salvaged, or donated. Sometimes wanting something over a period of time can lend even more meaning to finally getting it. This applies to acquiring your first mandolin, banjo, or whatever. Patience is a virtue in everything and no less so in learning to play music. If you develop a little patience while waiting to own your first musical instrument, it will come in handy while you're learning to play it.

It's more fun, it's easier, it's *better* when you learn music by osmosis—the same way that the walls of a plant's cells absorb water. (Did you know that music can affect the rates at which fluids pass through plant-cell walls and thus can affect the growth of the plant? See Chapter 10 of Peter Tompkins and Christopher Bird's book, *The Secret Life of Plants,* for more on this subject.) So *get close* to other musicians, even before you think you're ready to join in their jam sessions—especially before you're ready to carry your full weight in those sessions. Observe musicians as they play. Pay close attention to what they do and how they get the effects they get. Absorb their techniques.

And, even more important, open your awareness to the vibrations that musicians give off as they play. I know it may sound strange to folks who are just starting out, but I have a strong feeling that music is transmitted telepathically as well as through the ears. You can learn a lot more a lot faster from an accomplished musician—*and increase the energy level of whatever he or she is playing*—just by giving full attention to the tune and the performance.

Maybe this notion of mine isn't as strange as it sounds. Harmony is essentially rhythm, since a musical note has a regular vibration pattern and two or more notes played together must vibrate together to be harmonious. When two musical notes are played in harmony, the vibrations reinforce each other and make the sound stronger. Likewise, when one string on a stringed instrument is played, all other strings that are tuned in harmony with it will vibrate, too, even if they're not plucked. (This is called sympathetic vibration, and you can see it if you will watch the strings of a piano when you hit a note while pressing down on the sustain pedal. Surprise! Several strings vibrate, and the closer the sympathetically tuned strings are to the note you played, the more they will move.)

It's the same with people. Each individual is an energy source. So if you want to learn to play—vibrate—musically, put yourself close to others who play. Get in tune with what they're doing. Your active listening alone will increase the energy level of the tunes they're playing, and you'll begin to *feel* (not just listen to) the melodies, rhythms, emotions, and inflections that your friends are expressing.

One more thing: Always remember that it's the *music* that's important, not the technique. Not all of us play the same way, but it is our individuality that makes the world interesting. It's worthwhile to try to learn a particular technique from another player, but if it comes out sounding different when you play it, maybe you're developing your *own* technique! Just let your soul take over, and it will educate your mind.

Because it's the music that's important, I recommend that when you're getting started, you pick a song that you especially like and have a feeling for. Some books will try to teach you a particular song for the convenience of the author. It can be very hard to learn this way unless it's a song your heart wants to sing. To learn a song that means little to you is an intellectual exercise, but playing music is emotional. Find someone who knows a song you want to learn, or can figure it out for you. Or find a book that can teach you the song, or a record with that song on it. Write the song yourself if it can't be found by any of these methods. (There's a chapter on song-writing later in this book.)

Music is a temporal experience. It deals with time, both in rhythm and in the frequency of individual tones. One of the best techniques for learning music has to do with timing in another sense: Play when you feel like it. In a song, a musical rest is just as important an element to the sound as the notes. Another kind of musical rest, sleeping, actually brings improvement. When you try something requiring physical dexeterity, your brain will continue to absorb the information from that experiment after the work is done. In the same way, your ability to express yourself through music will increase with the passage of time as well as through actual practice. Remember that it takes time for your body to learn things, and don't become frustrated if progress is slow. Most of all, feel good. Have fun!

Front porch pickin'.

So the first three big steps to making music are these:

1. Stop telling yourself you can't do it.
2. Get hold of an instrument that's your own. (Making those built-in instruments

Getting close to John and Irene Ullman.

your own means getting control over them by using the to express *yourself* musically.)

3. Start playing for and with other people.

Great! Now start snappin' those fingers and clappin' those hands. Start singing along. Get a pair of spoons or make up some sandpaper blocks on the spot. Join in! That's what music—homegrown music—is really all about. Music is a magical connection: The more energy you add to the music, the stronger the connection and the more magical it will be.

2

Making Your Own Instruments

ONCE you've started making your own music, one way to save money and have a good time all at once is to make your own musical instruments at home. Here are a few ideas for doing just that without even going down to the local music store.

Blowing Your Mind on the Jug

You don't have to do anything to a jug to turn it into a musical instrument except empty it, at least partly. Old ceramic molasses jugs, (which, on occasion, have been known to be filled with other beverages, such as corn liquor) are, of course, the traditional ones for this use. Any kind of jug, from a half-gallon to a five-gallon one, will do the job, though.

A jug is properly played somewhat like a horn. That is, you do *not* use your lips and mouth to produce an ordinary pop-bottle whistle. In-

Larry "Mr. Jug" Van Over demonstrates the proper technique for playing the jug.

stead, press your lips together and blow air through them to make sort of a motorboat sound. When you direct this sound into the container, the jug resonates and amplifies it in somewhat the same way a guitar body resonates and amplifies the sound of its strings. Different tones can be produced by either tightening or loosening the lips and by blowing harder or softer. Experiment, too, with tipping the jug up and down to change the angle at which you direct air into it.

A good jug has a bass range that, to some degree, overlaps the range of the washtub. Its sound is kind of a cross between the pipe organ, the gutbucket, and the slide trombone. The effect is both musical and humorous, so get some folks together, pass the jug around, everybody practice his or her best tones, and see if you don't wind up having a hilarious evening.

The Kazoo

It doesn't take anything but a comb and some waxed paper to make your traditional down-home kazoo. Simply wrap the paper around the comb, press it to your lips, and hum a tune. You can cup your hands (the way a harmonica player does) around the instrument for a *wah-wah* effect. Other papers and techniques work, too. Experiment.

If you want to get a little fancier, commercially made kazoos are available from both music and toy stores (they're often less expensive at the toy shops). A few kazoos played in harmony make a great reed-and-brass section for any group of do-it-yourself musicians. And a marching kazoo band can liven up a dead church social, organization picnic, or other gathering when all else fails.

When the reed blows out on your store-bought kazoo, you can replace it with a bit of candy wrapper, cigarette package cellophane, or similar material. The way people throw that stuff around, you never have to look far for something to use. Also, nail clippers are a fairly good tool for trimming the reed to fit if you don't have scissors.

Commercially-made harmonica racks will also hold a kazoo so you can accompany yourself on guitar (or whatever). You don't need to spend your money, though—you can easily make a kazoo-holder from a good stiff coat hanger. If you make it just for a kazoo it might even work better than the harp rack. Just bend the bottom of the coat hanger into a U-shape to go around your neck. This "U" will then be roughly perpendicular to the original plane of the hanger. The hook of the hanger should be bent into a closed circle to hold your kazoo. (The kazoo can be taped in if necessary.) The final angle you hold your hummer at can then be adjusted to suit you.

The Spoons

Common, ordinary kitchen spoons are perhaps the most immediately available homemade instruments of all. Hold two of them back-to-back loosely in one hand, with your index finger between the handles (depending on the curvature of the spoons and the width of your fingers, you may need two fingers between), and let the bowls rattle together as you beat them between your knee and your other hand.

You can get interesting effects by playing a set of spoons in front of your open mouth as you change the size of the opening (in much the same way that you do when you play a jaw harp). Or you can run the spoons across the outstretched fingers of your other hand to get a trill. That's kind of like what you'd do on a washboard, except that here, the spoons make the sound.

Spoons can also be made to sound like castanets. I have a friend who sometimes switches off to a set of hand-carved wooden spoons, in addition to playing all sorts of metal ones. Each set has a sound all its own, so be sure you try the whole fleet. (Speaking of fleets, Marty Lepore of Seattle told me those nice heavy U.S. Navy issue spoons are his favorite.)

Scrubbin' Out Rhythm on the Washboard

This one is a natural for all you table-top drummers. Any washboard has possibilities for doubling as a portable trap set. While I prefer the tone of brass washboards, Jeff Hanna (a member of the Dirt Band, formerly known as the Nitty Gritty Dirt Band) swears by his own enameled steel model, which has a sharper tone than brass and, according to Jeff, lasts much longer than boards made of any other material. This may be true, since all the full-time washboard players I know wear out their brass boards in fairly short order. Players from Louisiana that I know—three of the living greats: Washboard Leo Thomas, Cleveland Chenier, and Wilbert Lewis—all use custom-made stainless-steel washboards, which may last even longer.

But as I've said, any kind you find can be used, though glass requires special treatment: You need to use plastic guitar finger picks instead of metal thimbles. If you can't find a good metal washboard around the old homestead or up in your grandmother's attic, figure on picking one up in a junk shop for around $15, maybe less. I've actually seen one homemade wooden washboard played by a member of the Gravity Adjusters Expansion Band (out of Sebastopol, California). The washboard was a couple of hardwood (rosewood) boards with grooves cut across their width. The boards were attached to a frame, along with various other items to plunk on.

When all else fails, it's still possible to purchase brand-new washboards—even brass ones! Several mail-order hardware outfits carry them.

The most common method of playing washboard percussion involves wearing metal thimbles on all of the fingers of one hand, if you hold the board with your other hand, or on both hands if you put a strap around your neck to hold the washboard while you play. I've even fashioned a couple of thumb picks out of sheet metal so my thumbs can dance as well! (Later I discovered that metal dobro guitar picks do exist for both left- and right-handed players, though they're hard to find.

Another advantage to the strap-around-the-neck system is that it makes it easier for you to play and dance at the same time. Believe me, a dancing washboard player is a sight to see! Most players don't stop at just playing the corrugated scrubbing surface, though. We add cowbells, pans, pan lids, wood blocks, bicycle bells, cymbals, tin cups—anything that adds an interesting sound. Some setups become so elaborate, they merit the title "washboard hootenanny" (a term reportedly coined by one Sheriff Tex, whose get-up has its own seat, includes two washboards, and is entirely chrome-plated).

Tod Parks of Snohomish, Washington. Notice the thimbles glued to the ends of the glove fingers.

Another improvement I discovered sort of by accident is that the tone can be changed by adding a back to the commercial washboard. I repaired a washboard with a bad frame by putting a back on it, and presto! The back changed the sound. Rich Kuras of Corvallis, Oregon (who told me about playing glass boards with plastic picks), adds a back of masonite to his boards, giving them a sharper sound and more projection. Projection isn't really a problem with the washboard, though. Even when I play mine with groups that use amplifiers, I don't need a microphone to be heard.

Various players use other methods for scrubbing out rhythm on the washboard. One player wrote that he plays with Dixieland groups using a spoon. Jeff Hanna told me he saw a fellow named Butch Wax using a plastic-handled hairbrush—scrubbing with the bristles and scraping the backside across. Another friend, Jerry Murry, told me the old Mountain Dew Jugband out of Montana used an industrial toilet-bowl brush! Cleveland Chenier uses several metal bottle openers on his custom stainless-steel washboard/vest, and Wilbert Lewis of Queen Ida and the Bon Temps Zydeco Band uses two stainless-steel meat hooks on his similar model. You get the idea that we all have our own individual style. You'll find yours, too! Just get hold of a washboard and start making rhythm.

If you use thimbles, you may find you have trouble keeping them on. I've discovered various methods of dealing with this problem. Some players will tape the thimbles to their fingers, if they expect to play all night. Jeff Hanna mashes his thimbles down to an oval shape with his teeth, to make them fit his fingers more tightly. Tod Parks, of Snohomish, Washington, has devised a clever method (with his wife's help, he says) for keeping them on *and* getting them off again fast when he switches to his other instrument. He glued his thimbles with epoxy to the ends of the fingers of a pair of lightweight cotton gloves. When a thimble finally did come off (years later), Tod says the hardened epoxy that remained worked just as well as the thimble.

My own method for getting thimbles on and off fast involves the use of a small plastic fishing-tackle box. I cut a block of ¾-inch lumber to fit the biggest bin in the top tray, then drilled holes to fit my thimbles. I arranged the holes in a pattern that makes it convenient to stick my fingers into all five thimbles at once. The other bins hold my harmonicas and finger picks, and underneath I keep guitar strings, a tuning fork, screwdrivers (these come in handy when one of my pipe-clamp cowbell-mounting brackets or similar devices gets loose), and such paraphernalia.

You certainly can be a one-man band if you mount a harmonica rack or similar device on the top of your board. Reggie Myles, an itinerant street-player on the Seattle-Santa Cruz-New Orleans circuit, puts out quite a sound with all the harps, kazoos, whistles, sirens, and other gadgets he has mounted on top of his rig. The name of the game is *inventiveness*.

When you're jumping into a jam with your scrub board at the ready, don't feel that fast ragtime sufff like "Coney Island Washboard" is the only music to get down with. Washboard rhythm works great on bluegrass, and I love to limber mine up on old rhythm and blues—which is the real basis for the zydeco (Cajun-Creole party music) of groups like Queen Ida and Clifton Chenier (Cleveland's brother). Swing is great, too. Try anything with a bit of rhythm to it.

A Festival of Saws

Back in the early part of this century, the beautiful, wailing sounds of musical saws were heard in many vaudeville shows and dance orchestras. Then along came all the various sophisticated Hawaiian, dobro, and pedal slide guitars, and the art of coaxing melodies from woodcutting hand tools was almost forgotten.

Today, I'm happy to report, musical saw playing is one "dying art" that is coming back to life. In fact, I've had the pleasure, twice, of attending the annual musical saw festival in Santa Cruz, California, a two-day gala event that is filled with the plaintive strains of the dual-purpose implement.

Those of you who happen to catch the playing bug (or who are already stricken) may wish to learn the dates for the next musical saw festival. To get that information, send a self-addressed, stamped envelope to Festival of the Saws (see the folk music publications list in the *Resources* section for the address). When the date is set, those folks will send you their newsletter. I guarantee that you'll have a good time if you're able to make it to the event. The festival usually features workshops for tub bass, bones, spoons, washboard, harmonica, kazoo, penny whistle, steel guitar, song-writing, and song-swapping, as well as beginning, intermediate, and advanced musical saw instruction.

YOU, TOO, CAN PLAY THE SAW!

Some of you may be wondering, "Just how difficult *is* musical saw playing?" The answer, surprisingly enough, is that it's really not at all hard to make music on a common, everyday board-tearing tool. The fact is that just about anyone can learn to rhapsodize on the cutting instrument, and that just about any handsaw can be turned into a tuneful tool.

That's right. You don't need some finely honed $600 instrument for this kind of down-home music-making. In fact, according to one famous saw player, Charlie Blacklock of Alameda, California, even a rusty old tool-shed reject might be a potential melody-maker.

Tom Scribner jamming with Hokum & Ragtime at the Saw Festival in Santa Cruz, California.

Since I used to be a carpenter by trade, I have access to a lot of handsaws, so I put Mr. Blacklock's statement to the test. And to tell the truth, I found that my rustiest junkyard saw was so marginally playable that trying to make sweet harmonies with it would probably prove frustrating to a beginner. (A good buffing job, however, might improve the tool's resonating qualities.) Other than that one, though, all the saws I tried, including an inexpensive, plastic-handled model, were playable.

Queen Ida with her brother Willie on his custom-made scrubboard.

As it turned out, my own favorite woodcutter, a Sandvik saw, was the best hardware-shelf musical instrument that I tested. (By the way, you can still use your tool for sawing *without* harming the musical properties. In fact, the more exercise your cutter gets, the more flexible and easy it'll be to play.)

Once you've scrounged up a good tune-maker, you'll need a striker (which is easy enough to make) to play your instrument with. Just drill a small hole in the side of a 2-inch piece of broomstick, glue a pencil (or a 5- or 6-inch length of ¼-inch dowel) into the opening to serve as a handle, and cover the head of the mallet with a ¼-inch-thick piece of felt or a felt washer. (A store-bought marimba mallet also works, if you can find one.)

HOW TO MAKE YOUR SAW SING

When all your equipment's ready, sit down and place the handle of the saw between your knees. Face the teeth toward your body (essential only if you intend to use a bow), slant the instrument at about a 45-degree angle (in other words, if you're right-handed, the handle of the saw should butt against your right knee), and hold the tip of the saw in your left hand (If you're a southpaw, you should, of course, reverse the instructions.)

Now exert pressure with the thumb of your left hand at a point about two inches down the blade while you pull up on the tip of the saw with your fingers. At the same time, bend the whole curved-between-thumb-and-fingers end of the saw away from you. This action will give the face of the tool a double curve, sort of like a very bottom-heavy S-shape, with the big, lower bulge of the blade curving toward your body.

To make a note, simply strike the metal just above the top of the big curve. If you want to produce high notes, bend the tip farther toward the floor and strike the blade farther out toward the end. To get lower notes, on the other hand, just bend the curved tip toward the ceiling and hit the blade nearer the handle.

Once you know how to play some notes, you'll be able to start sounding out easy tunes. Keep them slow and simple at first. The folks at Mussehl & Westphal, who make quality musical saws, suggest opening numbers such as "Home, Sweet Home" and "Aloha Oe," but I feel strongly that any person who starts to master a musical instrument should have the immediate gratification of playing music that he or she *likes*, so by all means feel free to try some of your own simple favorites.

While you're figuring out the first songs in your saw repertoire, you'll also want to learn how to produce the expressive, quavering sound effect known as *vibrato*. Most players quiver their saw-butt-holding leg to achieve the trembling quality. (To do this, plant your left leg squarely on the ground, while your right leg is up on toe like a ballet dancer's. Wobbling your right heel up and down produces the effect). A few, like master sawyer Tom Scribner, produce a vibrato effect by shivering the tip of the blade. Either way, if you practice long enough, you'll eventually perfect the technique.

After you've gotten some tune-making experience, you may want to replace the striking tone of the mallet with the continuous sound that a saw can produce when it's played with a bow. You can use a simple homemade string-player (like a young child's arrow-shooting toy) or go the high-class and finer-sounding route and use a real live fiddle or cello bow (most pros use cello bows, which have more surface area and can produce louder tone more easily). In either case, work a good layer of rosin—the substance all violinists use—on the bow before you start to play.

Then simply draw the sound-evoker across the edge of the saw in the same places that you would strike with the hammer. I've observed that in actual practice the pros will slide the bow up the edge a bit while stroking, rather than draw straight across one point, in order to cross the exact point that sets the saw singing. Although you may need to bear down a little initially to set the saw vibrating, be sure to let up on the pressure as soon as you can, or your bow strings won't last long.

Since the saw is a melody instrument and has no fixed notes, you'll find it's a lot easier to play against a background of chords on guitar, piano, or accordion. If you can't find someone to play with, you can play along with records. But it shouldn't be too awfully hard to find someone who can chord for you.

EXPERIENCED SAW PLAYING

You may also, after a while, decide you're ready to move up to the professional league and buy a genuine made-for-music saw. Such instruments will produce more volume than most hardware-store crooners, and because they're a couple of inches longer than ordinary saws, they have a greater range, too, sometimes as much as two octaves.

You may even be lucky enough to find a classic old musical saw, such as the gold-plated, rhinestone-encrusted 1921 Mussehl & Westphal or the Sandvik "Stradivarius" model, at a secondhand store. (One of my neighbors recently did just that!) If not, you can write off for information about purchasing either a Mussehl & Westphal or a C. Blacklock

John Walkup performing on the saw with piano accompanist.

Special, available from Charlie Blacklock himself (see the *Resources* section on mail-order houses for the addresses). Be sure to send a self-addressed, stamped envelope when asking for information from either of these small companies.

The M&W saw is made from English steel and comes complete with three pages of instructions, a mallet, a dowel bow, a string bow, extra string, a rosin cake, and a vinyl carrying case. But you can buy just the saw, if you don't want the paraphernalia.

Charlie Blacklock worked out a special arrangement with San Jose's Valley Saw Company for the manufacture of his musical woodcutters, because that firm uses what he considers to be the most tuneful material available: Swedish steel. There is a difference, though I would be hard put to state a preference. But then, I like many different types of music, too!

Washtub Bass Variations

Any homemade music—whether hammered out on the piano, guitar, banjo, fiddle, or whatever—becomes more interesting and more fun for everyone as more and more instruments are added to the festivities, especially if those instruments contribute some tonal and rhythmic coloring of their own. One of the basic additions you can make to any pickin' and grinnin' group is the down-home washtub bass, or "gutbucket." Although the instrument's main contribution is solid rhythmic accompaniment, it can produce true notes (much to the amazement of electric-bass players) with a range of about an octave and a half.

Start this construction project by scrounging up a No. 1, 2, or 3 washtub or similar large metal container. Don't settle for one with the bottom rusted out because to be a musical instrument, a tub has to have a strong bottom. Buy a new tub if you have to. It won't break you. A new No. 1 washtub costs only about $15.

The neck for your gutbucket should be approximately 4½ feet long, and it can be anything from a whittled-down hardwood sapling to an old rake handle or even a piece of steel conduit attached to the tub with a strap hinge. I'm using a piece of an old wheelbarrow handle for mine. The stronger the neck of your instrument, the better, since lighter ones tend to absorb string vibrations and dampen a gutbucket's sound.

But where do you buy strings for it? That all depends on what you decide to use for strings. The range of choices is wide. Some musicians swear by the unwrapped gut A string made for the bass viol. Depending on the size of tub you use, though, a D or a G may be more appropriate. You can order these strings through a music store or from some of the sources listed in the mail-order section of *Resources*. Another camp favors the steel-string sound that you can get either with piano wire or with 1/16-inch stainless-steel aircraft cable. These steel-string varieties have to be attached differently, as I'll explain later.

I've also seen a braided nylon line, kind of like parachute-shroud line, used. Hardware stores have this type of thing. A compromise between the nylon- and steel-string sounds is found in plastic-coated, steel-core clothesline, which you can buy at your local supermarket. For a couple of bucks you can get a year's supply. This stuff wears out faster than piano wire, aircraft cable, and braided nylon, but it's cheap and it works. The bass player in my band uses it exclusively.

Attach the string to the center of the upside-down washtub by one of two methods:

1. Drill a hole a little larger than the string in the bottom of the tub, thread the string through the opening, and knot the line on the inside of the tub to hold it in place, or

2. Bolt a small hasp or eye bolt to the center of the bottom of the tub and tie your string to it.

With either method, it's advisable to reinforce the inside bottom of the container with something like a peanut butter jar lid, a circle of sheet metal, or a circle of ¼-inch plywood. You can cement the reinforcing disc in place or just let the knotted string or eye bolt hold it there like a big washer. It's also a good idea—if you use the knotted-string method—to pass the line through a couple of fiber washers first, then through the reinforcing disc, and to tape the string where it passes through the metal bottom of the tub—all to protect the line from wearing out from rubbing against metal.

If you use a wooden pole for the neck of your gutbucket, notch the bottom end of the pole so it can be hooked over the little rim that runs around the bottom of the washtub. Then bevel off the side of the notch that faces the bottom of the tub so it won't touch the metal (and dampen the tone) as the neck is leaned back and forth during a song.

Drill a hole a little larger than your string through the neck of the gutbucket about 5 inches down from the top (to leave a nice handle to hold on to; if you don't feel you need that much handle, cut your stick 3 or 4 inches shorter). You may also want to bevel off the outside edges of this hole to prevent the string from wearing out.

OK, pass the string through the hole and adjust it so that it pulls taut when the string is standing straight up and the stick is leaning over the tub. Then wind the string around the neck and tie it above the hole, and you're ready to play!

Hold the washtub down by planting your foot (left foot for southpaws, right for the rest of us) on the tub rim opposite of where your pole rests. And make sure that foot rests

Homegrown musicians, featuring the washtub bass. (The ax is a gag.)

only on the rim of the tub — otherwise you'll deaden the gutbucket's sound.

Some players like to rest the far side of the tub on something like a two-by-four to let the sound out. You can cut grooves in this board, or nail blocks to it to prevent the tub from walking off it while you're playing that walking bass line. Other players will drill a hole about 7/8-inch in diameter in the side of the tub to act as an air vent, so that the tub doesn't restrict the sound. I've also heard of cutting large sound vents in front of the tub.

Nearly all players remove the handles of the washtub so they won't rattle in the middle of a hot song. The old-fashioned tubs, if you can find one at a secondhand store or somewhere, are made of heavy-guage metal and have wooden handles. I've been told that these old tubs make good instruments, and you don't have to remove the handles. Bruce Bratton, of Santa Cruz, California, leaves one of his metal handles on in order to stand on it, thus preventing the tub from walking away as he's playing. Bruce also recommends the No. 5 eye-hoe handle as the optimum neck for a tub bass.

During the actual strumming, just pull back or let up on the gutbucket's stick with one hand (to change the instrument's pitch) while you pluck that single string with the other. And when you're ready to wail, make sure your group tackles a song in which you get to play a solo!

WINGING IT WITH AIRCRAFT CABLE

I picked up some more good ideas on gutbucket design from Jimmie Fadden of the Dirt Band. Although his fans probably know Jimmie for his stellar harmonica work—particularly his performance on "Will The Circle Be Unbroken"—he used to play the tub bass back when the group was just a fledgling jug band. Jimmie said he learned his design from Fritz Richmond of the immortal Jim Kweskin Jug Band.

The main feature of Richmond's instrument design is the use of 1/16-inch stainless steel aircraft cable for string. The strong filament, which can be bought ready-made with a steel ball attached to one end, is secured to the tub bottom by a scrounged bicycle-brake adjuster. First, drill an appropriate-size opening in the center of the bottom of your washtub. Then pass the aircraft cable through the open shaft of the bike part and fit it into the hole. Attach the unit to the bottom of the tub with a plywood washer 2 inches in diameter

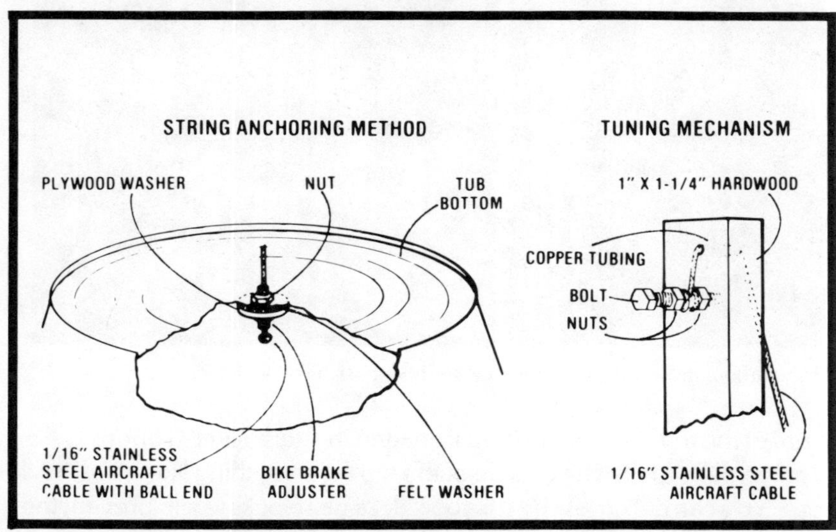

Fig. 1 Fritz Richmond's tub design.

that is glued to a matching felt washer. Last of all, tighten the whole assembly—on the outside of the floor of the tub, using the nut that came with the brake adjuster (see Fig. 1 for details).

At the opposite end of the cable—near the top of the neck of the instrument—Jimmie uses a length of small-diameter copper tubing to reinforce the hole where the string passes through the neck. And to make a secure tuning machine, he uses a bolt with a hole drilled in the center large enough to accommodate the cable. He fastens two nuts to the bolt (one on either side of the cable), and screws the whole unit into the side of the neck. Then, when he tunes his bass, the string will wrap around the bolt and stay clamped between the nuts permanently. (With the commonly used wrapped-and-knotted clothesline, the string tends to slip and has to be retied occasionally.)

In the earlier part of this chapter I mentioned only one method of getting different notes out of your gutbucket: adjusting the string tension by pulling back or letting up on the string. Actually, some players—Jimmie Fadden included—fret their instrument, or shorten the string length by sliding their hand down the neck and grasping the string tightly to the pole. Others will use this method only to get a sort of capo effect—they hold the stick and string in a different spot to play in a higher key. In either case, you might benefit from another of the tips Jimmie passed on to me: During his gutbucket stomp days, Jimmie wore a heavy canvas glove on his nonpicking hand, with a strip of thick leather sewn across the fingers at the point where they touched the string. He says that a groove quickly wears into the leather, making it easy to maintain that same point of contact. If you use this technique, you might like to follow Jimmie's example further and cut off the ends of the fingers of the glove for natural air conditioning.

Furthermore, if you're going to play tub bass during a long jam session, you might want to wrap your plucking fingers with adhesive tape to keep them from blistering.

A NEW TUB DESIGN

Another design I'd like to pass along was described to me by Kevin Potter, who read my column in *The Mother Earth News*. He calls the invention an upright washtub bass. It's essentially a banjo-style version of the bull fiddle, and it uses the tub for the pot. (See Fig. 2.)

Kevin's creation is a hybrid instrument made partly from scrounged pieces and partly from components of a conventional bass fiddle. The neck of the music-maker is a hardwood push-mower handle, and the stand can be a chair leg or a table leg. The fiddle's tuning peg, bridge, and string are the same as those used on a "real" instrument. Kevin and I agree that it is possible to make the same pieces out of any good hardwood scraps and that the string could be nylon filament, or even clothesline.

You'll need a length of wood 2-by-3-inches for a back support—actually, any board that's close to those dimensions will work, as long as it comfortably spans the diameter of the top of the tub when laid across it. You'll also need a U-shaped brace, which can be welded out of scraps of steel or angle iron. Make the open end of this brace straddle the neck of the instrument, and bolt it to the neck. Lag-bolt the closed end through the tub into one end of the back support.

Attach the mower-handle neck to the tub with wood screws and a small angle bracket. You'll also need one turnbuckle per string, a double-ended screw to secure the chair leg in place (if the leg didn't come with one of its own), and a small piece of hardwood to use as a nut where the strings rest at the top of the neck.

You can make the holes to hold your tuning peg in one of two ways. Kevin used six drill bits of diminishing size, boring about 1/4 inch at a time with each successively smaller bit. Another, equally effective way to make the conical hole is to make the first bore with the smallest-size bit, then enlarge the opening with a repairman's tapered hand reamer, a tool that is available at most hardware stores. Violin-makers use a similar tool called a peg-hole reamer, the taper of which is more gradual than that of the repairman's tool (as is the store-bought tuning peg). If you use the repairman's reamer, you should whittle your own peg with a similar taper.

Bolt the turnbuckle tailpiece in place through a hole drilled in the bottom rim of the tub.

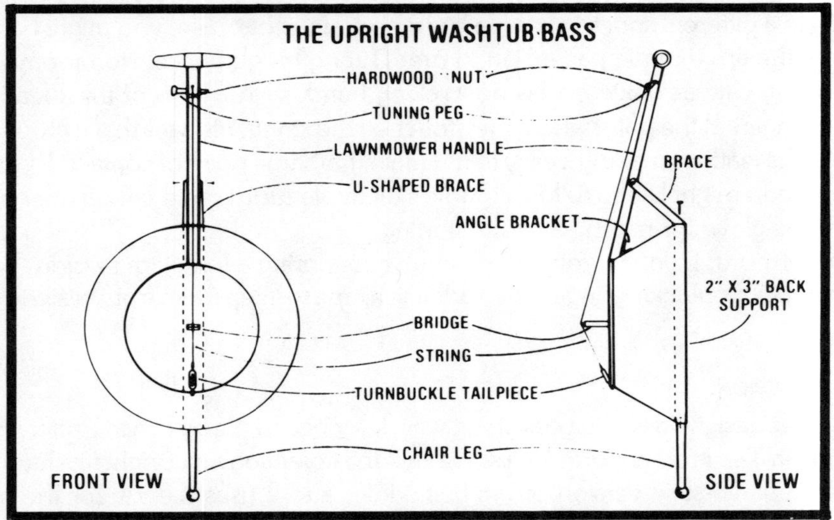

Fig. 2

As you can see from Fig. 2, the neck tilts slightly backward from the edge of the drum, allowing for a taller bridge, which must be set at a height that will keep the string almost parallel to the neck because—as a general rule—the higher the bridge, the more resonance and volume your instrument will produce, particularly in the bass range. If you buy a standard bridge, of course, the dimensions of that store-bought part will determine the neck angle.

The great advantage of Kevin's innovative design is that it gives you the option of adding extra strings to the instrument to extend its tonal range. It's even possible to make a four-string upright tub bass, but if you do, you'll need to use a wider piece of wood for the neck. The instrument is played like a real bull fiddle (not like the regular gutbucket) and it can also be bowed, if it's fitted with more than two strings, after you've reshaped the neck to match a commercially manufactured bridge.

THE AMAZING ELECTRIC WASHTUB BASS

Another *Mother Earth News* reader, William Boothe of Newport News, Virginia, was inspired to build a tub bass from Kevin Potter's design, and went on to make some improvements of his own. For one thing, he added frets to his two-string model. These frets are simply galvanized staples that you can locate by rigging some sort of movable fret (like a nail with a rubber band around the back). Bill also braced his table-leg stand with four aluminum braces, secured at the tub end with felt washers to eliminate rattling. For position markers, the wily Mr. Boothe used red-headed tacks, and he developed his own combination tailpiece bridge complete with adjustable saddles for the strings. To top the whole concoction off Bill added a bathroom plunger end to the bottom, to prevent the instrument from slipping, and an electric guitar pickup on the inside. Just goes to show what you can do if you're a bit inventive!

Yet another version of the washtub bass, this one featuring a wood top and electric bass tuners. It's pictured with its creator, Ted Jones, of Oroville, Washington.

Quentin Rhoton, bass player with the Okie Doke Band (the outfit I've been playing with for the last six years or so) has discovered that the best way to amplify a tub bass for performing with other amplified instruments is to use the same kind of transducer-type contact pickup sold for use on upright basses. These units generally come with a preamplifier, and can be plugged into an ordinary electric bass amplifier or straight into a microphone input on a P.A. mixing board.

Going Bonkers on a Homemade Box Drum

Mother Earth News reader Irene Scyriver wrote me not long ago to ask for information about building a "mystery drum," which she described as "an oblong wooden box with a grooved surface that's played with padded sticks."

As luck would have it, soon after I received Irene's letter, I happened to hear a Seattle musician, Mark Filler, playing such an instrument (he called it a "tongue drum") on a local live radio show. So I contacted Mark and got the whole scoop on these unusual percussion music-makers.

It seems that the wooden instruments go by any number of names. There have been similar instruments in both Africa and South America, and both places have literally hundreds of separate native languages. Since the sound the drum makes is much like the word "bonk" (and because we'll be talking about building our own drums and ought to be able to call them what we like), I've chosen the name "bonker box." Here's how to make one for yourself.

IF I HAD A HAMMER

To begin, gather a supply of 3/4-inch planks. The lumber that will be used for the *top* of the box—which is the sounding surface— should be hardwood, such as oak or Honduras mahogany (oak planks can be scrounged from pallet boards or even junked furniture). You shouldn't have much trouble locating this material at a reasonable price. After all, small sections of lumber are pretty easy to come by (and most bonkers are around a foot long, while the biggest I've seen was only 27 inches in length). Hold your chosen board by a corner and rap it with a knuckle. If it rings, you've got yourself a good one!

The planks used on the sides and bottom of the instrument are not as important as material for the top. Just remember that harder wood will generally produce a brighter tone.

As you may have guessed, bonker-box dimensions can vary considerably. The size of your drum will be determined by how you plan to play the instrument. Since the base of the box should never rest on a solid surface while you're playing music (that dampens the tone considerably), a small unit, which can be cradled between your knees, is the best bet. If you decide to make a large drum, build a stand for it, or at least set the box up on strips of rubber or felt so the whole box can ring out.

Although it's possible to construct a bonker box with the simplest of hand tools, you'll find it easier to get tight joints (and superior sound) if you use a table saw and a jointer. Folks who don't happen to have the appropriate tools may be able to barter with a local handyman for the labor or buy the boards from a lumberyard that'll cut them to shape. Those of you who have no wish to design your own bonker boxes see Fig. 3, which shows the dimensions for two sample drums.

The slots in the top of the drum, which separate the tongue-shaped keys, can be made with a drill and a jigsaw or sabre saw. Each tongue should be 1 to 1 1/2 inches wide, and the margins around the keys, on all four sides, should be of similar (but not necessarily identical) width. The long margins will produce tones of their own on drums with a slit along the side of the box, so you may want to make these margins of unequal width to increase the range of your instrument. Mark off the proposed cuts with pencil lines running lengthwise. If your top is to be 6 inches wide, for example, you might draw the first line 1 3/8 inches from the edge, the next line 1 1/2 inches from the first line, and another line 1 1/2 inches farther over, which should leave a 1 5/8-inch margin on the far side. (The

some sample bonker box specs

For a small drum:
TOP AND BOTTOM: 11-3/4" X 5-1/4" X 3/4"
SIDES: 11-3/4" X 3-1/2" X 3/4"
ENDS: 3-3/4" X 3-1/2" X 3/4"
The tongues—laid out to be 1-1/2" wide—are 3" and 6-1/4" in length on one strip, while the other pair of keys are 4-1/4" and 5" long respectively. The margins around the tongues are 1-1/4" at each end, 1-1/4" on one "long" side, and 1" along the other lengthwise edge. The side-piece slots should be 8-1/2" long beneath the edge with the wider margin, and 6-1/2" long on the opposite side.

For a larger drum:
TOP AND BOTTOM: 18" X 7-1/2" X 3/4"
SIDES: 18" X 7-1/2" X 3/4"
ENDS: 7-1/2" X 6" X 3/4"
The six tongues are 1-1/4" wide, and pair up in lengths of 3-1/2" and 8-1/2", 4-3/4" and 7-1/4", and 5-3/4" and 6-1/4" . . . based upon 12" slots. Your end margins should be 3", while one side will have a 2" border and the other an "edge" 1-3/4" wide. The narrow-margined side is turned into a sounding surface through the use of a 9" slot, while the remaining "seam" will have a slit of 11" in length.

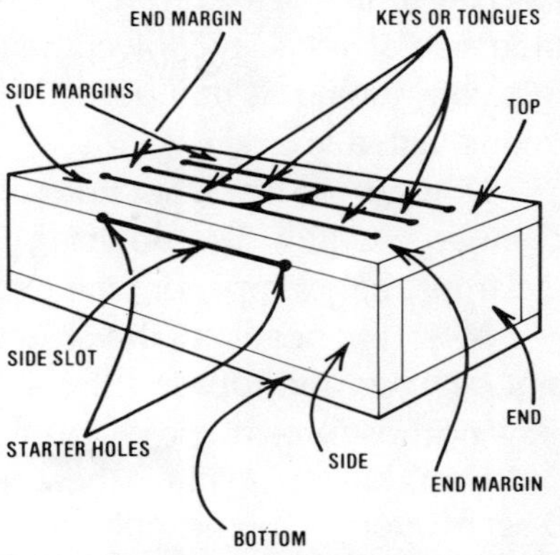

END MARGIN
KEYS OR TONGUES
SIDE MARGINS
TOP
SIDE SLOT
END
STARTER HOLES
SIDE
END MARGIN
BOTTOM

Fig. 3

space between cuts will be diminished by the width of your saw blade, of course, perhaps by as much as 1/8 inch.)

Now draw a line at each end of the board perpendicular to your lengthwise lines to mark the short outside borders of your musical tongues. Be sure that these end margins are at least as wide as those on the sides. Drill 3/8-inch starter holes for your saw blade in the six places where the two sets of lines intersect. Then use the saw to cut a narrow slot along each lengthwise pencil line between each pair of holes.

To determine the length of the tongues of the instrument, first mark the center point of the long slots. You're going to slice *across* each band (the long, narrow strip between the slots) at a point that is slightly off center, and at a different point on each band. If you saw across one band 1/4 inch from the center mark, you'll produce two tongues, one of which will be 1/2 inch longer than the other. If you make your other cut 1/2 inch off center, one of the two tongues produced will be a full inch longer than the other.

Depending on the width of your box top, you may have either two or three sets of keys. In order for each note - maker to produce a different pitch, no two tongues should be of equal length, so your second cut will be farther off center than the first, and the third (if you have three) farther off center than the second.

Remember that the above tongue lengths are no more than suggestions. You might, for example, actually *tune* the instrument if you can determine what length tongue will produce a specific note, but, since the sound will vary from one piece of wood to the next, I can't give you a formula for tuning your drum. A precision drum would likely require the use of expensive, imported hardwoods. The sequence of notes could probably be worked out mathematically so you would know how long to make each tongue. But I find that the oak-top drums with random tuning are more percussive than deliberately tuned bonker boxes, and a whole lot more versatile.

With the tongues cut and shaped, it's time to rout or chisel a groove crosswise on the underside of each tongue 1/4 to 1/2 inch wide and a little less than half the depth of the wood. The grooves will be like tiny troughs that run from starter hole to starter hole and give the keys additional freedom of movement, which will mean louder tones and will also affect the tuning of the drum. (You can raise the tone of a tongue by taking material off the underside of its tip, and lower the tone by increasing the depth of the groove at its base.) Test your tuning as you go by holding the drum top near your ear and rapping each tongue with a knuckle.

Now cut the five other sides of your box to size and make sure that all of your parts fit together snugly before applying yellow carpenter's glue to the joints. Then use large C-clamps, bar clamps, or pipe clamps to hold the assembly together while it dries.

Most, but not all, of the drums I've seen have had additional slots cut just below the joint between the top and the sides. These slots free the borders of the drum head, allowing those areas to produce percussive tones of their own.

Don't attempt to make these side cuts until the assembly has been glued *and* had time to set properly. Then simply drill a pair of starter holes 3/8 inch in diameter at the joint between the side panel and the drum top, and connect the holes by cutting along the seam with a sabre saw. You can vary the length of these slots, remembering that a longer cut will produce a lower tone.

There are several ways to make drumsticks for your homegrown instrument. Chopsticks, topped with 3/4-inch-in-diameter hard rubber super balls (the high bouncers that can be found in most any toy store) are almost ideal. Just drill a hole in each ball slightly smaller than the diameter of your stick and fasten the two parts together with contact cement. (It might also be prudent to cover each of these energetic spheres with a square of chamois, wrapping the overlap to the stick with a rawhide thong to keep the ball from taking flight during a hot solo — unless you're trying to bring down the house!)

SUPPORT YOUR LOCAL CRAFTSPERSON

Should you be interested in owning a bonker box but lack either the time, ambition, or mechanical ability to build your own, there are two craft houses that sell the drums in a variety of sizes. Furthermore, many of the home-business-made bonkers feature extra decoration and top-quality, exotic hardwood construction. Catalogs are available from Buckhorn Mountain Woodcrafts and from Hum Drums. (See the list of mail-order houses in the *Resources* section for addresses.) Be sure to include a self-addressed, stamped envelope with your request for information from either of these two outfits.

Playing Sweet Tunes on the Dulcimer

The Appalachian (or lap) dulcimer is often and enthusiastically promoted as one of the simplest places to start in either playing or building a stringed instrument. I have reservations about going into music with an "I'm-not-very-musical-so-I'll-get-a-dulcimer-because-they're-the-easiest-to-play" attitude. Think of yourself as plenty musical, and choose the instrument that you enjoy most. Choose the dulcimer if you love the sound of one.

There's a steadily growing group of dulcimer musicians in American folk music today. Many of these new artists have been experimenting with, and stretching the limits of, the mountain dulcimer's capabilities. Plucking simple single-note melodies is a good place to begin, but chances are that learning such advanced techniques as chording up the neck and finger-picking may prove to be even *more* rewarding.

So, if you've decided to take up dulcimer playing, *do* think of it as an easy place to get started in string music, but also set your sights on the horizon. You'll find that a lot more is possible with this uncomplicated instrument than playing "Mary Had A Little Lamb."

The Appalachian dulcimer is traditionally played sitting down, with the instrument resting across the lap. Notes are fretted either with the fingers of the left hand or with a noter stick while the right hand strums with a pick, or perhaps a feather quill (left-handers can reverse this). The traditional instrument has three strings — one that's used to play the melody, and two drones. More modern versions sometimes have a pair of unison-tuned strings for melody, which means the strings are tuned to the same note and placed close together to be fretted as one.

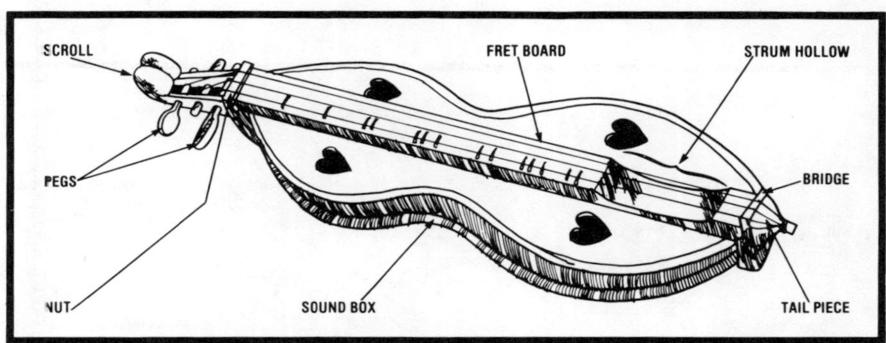

Fig. 4 An Appalachian dulcimer.

Most common lap dulcimers are either hourglass or teardrop shaped (see Fig. 4). Other designs are possible, though, and occasionally you'll see a "courting dulcimer," which is actually two music-makers in one. (The man and the woman play facing each other, with the instrument across both their laps.) Some of today's dulcimer players add a neck strap to the instrument, and play it standing up. And many accomplished players now fret whole chords, fingering all of the strings in the process. (See the *Song Section* for some chord diagrams.)

MAKING A HAMMERED DULCIMER

The name *dulcimer* has been applied to the small fretted instrument for only around the last 200 years. As long ago as biblical times, it referred to a hammered instrument. Since the word literally means "sweet tune" — and both instruments do, indeed, produce mellifluous tones — perhaps some old mountaineer plucked the name out of the Good Book and attached it to the Appalachian melody-maker.

The large hammered music box is a forerunner of the piano, but the pounding pieces that strike the strings are held in the player's hands instead of being built into the instrument's body and mechanically operated as the hammers on a piano are. Many countries throughout Europe and Asia have traditional versions of the hammered dulcimer — and a great many styles of music are played on them—but the basic form of the ancient instrument is nothing more than a trapezoidal sound box that has several groups (or *courses*) of strings that pass over a support (or *side bridge*) at one end of the instrument, across an off-center *mid-bridge*, and over another support to the other end. Some dulcimers have two central bridges, the second holding an extra set of bass strings. The mid-bridge is a distinctive trait of the hammered dulcimer and distinguishes the instrument from its ancestor, the psaltery.

As you can see from Fig. 5, a homemade hammered dulcimer can be built from scraps of dimensional lumber and plywood. You will probably need to purchase tuning pegs (old piano pegs will work), a tuning wrench (a hardware-store tapping chuck should serve the purpose), and a supply of No. 7 or No. 8 music wire (available from most music stores, hobby shops, and mail-order music supply houses; see the mail-order section of *Resources*).

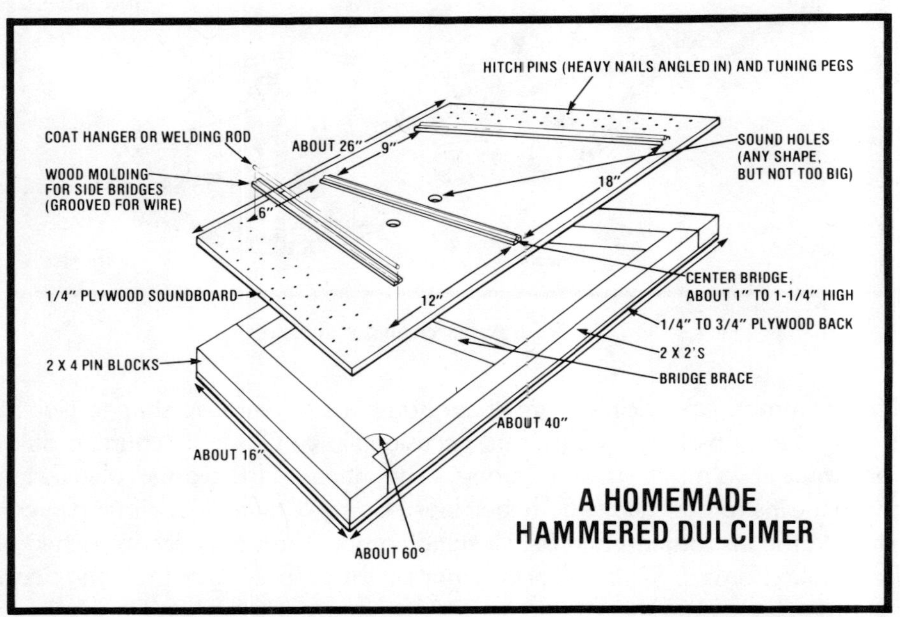

Fig. 5

Secure the top and back of the instrument with a good wood glue, then nail them in place. (Be sure to avoid putting any of the nails where the tuning pegs will later be installed.) Wrap each string around a tuning peg three or four times, lay it over the off-center bridge, loop it around a hitch pin on the opposite, and run it back to another peg on the original side. Every wire then forms two strings, and each pair will give one note on the right side of the main bridge and another (a fifth higher) on the left side of the divider.

One standard tuning for a 12-course hammered dulcimer—running from low notes at the bottom of the instrument to high ones at the top—is G-sharp, A, B, C-sharp (just above middle C), D, E, F-sharp, G, A, B, C, and D on the left side of the bridge; and

C-sharp, D, E, F-sharp, G, A, B, C, D, E, F, and G on the right side of the bridge. You'll have to adjust the new instrument several times over a period of days before it'll settle down and stay (more or less) in tune.

There are two pamphlets available with more detailed instructions for building hammered dulcimers. One, called "The Hammered Dulcimer Compendium," is available from the Blue Ridge Dulcimer Shop (under mail-order houses in *Resources*). The other, called "Making a Hammered Dulcimer," by Sam Rizetta, a prominent hammered dulcimerist, is available free from Public Inquiry Mail, Smithsonian Institution, Dept. MB, Washington, D.C. 20560. (You may wish to request a copy of "Hammered Dulcimer History and Playing," also by Sam Rizetta, from the Smithsonian Institution as well.)

DULCIMER KIT MANUFACTURERS

I'm not going to make an attempt here to list all the many kit manufacturers. The best thing to do for a complete listing is pick up a copy of *Frets* or one of the other folk music magazines (listed in the *Resources* section) and check out the advertisements. You can

Three kit instruments, left to right: the Fiddle Kit, from the Fiddle Works; the Tennessee Teardrop, from Hank Levin; a cardboard dulcimer, from Backyard Music.

also refer to the list of mail-order houses in the *Resources* section for names of dulcimer kit companies that I can recommend.

Making "Real" Instruments from Scratch

Most homegrown musicians dream at one time or another of building their own guitars or mandolins or banjos completely from scratch. And since the publication of the first modern book on the subject (*Classic Guitar Construction*, by Irving Sloan, E.P. Dutton, 1966), increasing numbers of folks have been building their own music-makers. In fact, it seems that all the do-it-yourself movement needed to really catch fire was some how-to information. When Mr. Sloan provided the necessary data instructions, homegrown craftsfolk started turning up everywhere.

One sure sign of the number of people who are building their own is the fact that there's now an organization, the Guild of American Luthiers, with over 1,300 members, that functions as an information-sharing forum for "luthiers." Tim Olson, a founder of the Guild and editor of its quarterly magazine, defines *luthier* as "a person who handmakes any instrument," although the term was originally applied only to lute builders. (Tim doesn't limit his definition to folks who work without the aid of power tools, but he *does* insist that a true luthier carries out each and every step in the construction.)

It costs $10 to join the organization, and all members receive the *Guild Quarterly* magazine, which contains how-to construction and repair articles along with news on the luthier scene around the country, advertisements (rates are half-price for members, and the classifieds are *free*), and some intriguing "et cetera." You can write to the organization in care of the magazine (see the folk music publications listing in the *Resources* section for the address).

3

Acquiring and Recycling Used Instruments

WHETHER you're just a homegrown music beginner or you've been playing for some time, the chances are good that you have been, are, or someday will be in the market for a used instrument. I'd like to share a few ideas and experiences that can help you in your hunt.

Perhaps the best way to get an old instrument is to have it handed down to you from a previous generation or owner. And even though you may not need any special talent to be so blessed, it certainly doesn't hurt to advertise your desire for such a gift.

Yes, advertise! Tell *all* your relatives and friends—tell everyone you meet—that you'd appreciate the donation of any old musical instrument in any condition at any time. The truth is that there are uncounted millions of guitars, fiddles, drums, accordions, or whatever, slowly rotting away right now in closets, attics, garages, and basements all over the country. Some haven't been played for years. Most are owned by people who don't care about them anymore, or who've even forgotten that they exist. All of these instruments have souls that are crying out to be reborn through the magic of your touch! So look around and ask around. I guarantee you'll get a response.

I once was given a beautiful old mandolin and a fiddle by a man who'd had them for 50 years. He picked me (and my guitar case) up when I was hitchhiking one day, and in the conversation that followed I mentioned that I was learning a little bit about stringed-instrument repair. One thing led to another, and before I knew it, I was the proud owner of two more old (but new to me) pieces of equipment. Although the fiddle needed new strings and hardware (tailpiece, bridge, and sound post), plus some minor regluing on the top and back, the mandolin (a rare 12-string "potato bug" model) sounded pretty good with nothing but a new set of strings. I've also discovered several guitars (usually in great need of repair) in barns, basements, garages, and sheds, after people who had heard of my interest in searching for such finds invited me in to have a look.

Of all the guitars I've turned up in my scavenging, only one has yet to make music again. And that's simply because I haven't found the time to fix it. Or maybe I just haven't worked up the courage. The instrument, which once did a hitch as an ivy planter before being stashed away in the corner of a barn, was full of dirt and had a couple of cracks in its top when I discovered it.

If you acquire musical instruments through any of my "ask-around, look-in-old-barns, scout-the-church-charity-shops" methods, most of the equipment you turn up will naturally be in need of repair. This need may be something as simple as a new set of strings, a new reed, or a drumhead. But it may be something that requires work by somebody who has had experience doing it.

Now I'm not saying you can't handle the job, but—at least in the beginning—I do recommend that you seek advice before you tackle any major renovation. You can ask people who have played the particular instrument a long time or professional repair people. In some cases, you can find the instructions you need in books (see the *Resources* section on construction and repair manuals).

A fiddlemaker's table at the Tumwater Bluegrass Festival. (Clarence Kelley of Vantage, Washington, is at center.)

New Life for an Old Slide Guitar

The first guitar I ever owned was one I found in a shed at my grandparents' place. I was told that this type of guitar was meant to be played on the lap, using a steel bar on the strings. Not ever having seen such a thing, I tried to learn to fret chords on it, achieving mostly frustration. Years later, in talking with guitar-playing friends, I learned that the

"Hawaiian guitar" was wildly popular in the teens, 20s, and 30s, with the result that thousands of lap-style guitars (and accompanying instruction books) were sold by mail order throughout the North American continent. You can still frequently run across them in secondhand stores, thrift shops, and attics.

Legend has it that in the 1890s a Hawaiian named Joseph Kekuku discovered this style of playing while humming through a comb-and-tissue-paper kazoo with his guitar resting in his lap. The comb slipped from his hand onto the guitar strings, creating a new sound, which Joseph immediately made again deliberately, much to his delight and our ultimate benefit. Guitars had been brought to Hawaii by Mexican and Portuguese settlers (cowboys, actually) much earlier. Hawaiian people had a long musical tradition, but it was primarily of vocal music, with some drum and seashell-whistle accompaniment. The Hawaiians took to tuning their guitars to an "open," or sung, chord, which simplified both chording and tuning by ear. This style of tuning in Hawaii is known as "slack key," because some strings are tuned down from standard to achieve the open chord.

With the guitar tuned in an open chord, a person can simply lay one finger straight across the fret board to make a different major chord. By sliding a steel bar up and down the neck the player can create a lot of different chords and sliding notes that will dazzle all listeners with audible visions of palm trees swaying in a tropical breeze!

It was this same Hawaiian-guitar fad that supplanted the musical saw in the dance orchestras of the 20s, and went on to become the trademark of modern "country" music in the form of the pedal steel guitar. The evolution from slide guitar to steel guitar happened this way:

At first lap-guitar players used ordinary guitars modified with a raised nut, which kept the strings high enough to prevent the steel bar from running into the frets. Early players used all sorts of things like metal combs, pocketknives, and flat metal bars of steel or brass. After World War I companies began manufacturing special lap guitars with hollow necks. The idea was that the extra space would improve the sound somehow. Then in 1926 the Dopera brothers invented the resonator guitar, which projected its very loud, distinctive sound through an inverted metal cone much like the cone of a loudspeaker, sustaining notes much longer than ordinary wooden guitars. Some of these resonator guitars were made entirely of metal except for the neck and bridge. The Dopera brothers eventually started their own guitar manufacturing company called Dobro. Their designs so dominated the market that resonator guitars became known as "dobro" guitars, whether manufactured by the Dopera brothers or not.

The dobro guitar was quickly adapted to use in Hawaiian steel-guitar playing. Coinciding with technological breakthroughs in recording, this guitar style became the first musical craze to sweep the nation, so that from its beginning, the sound became absorbed into other musical traditions.

By the time the Hawaiian music trend began to slow down in the 40s, the steel-guitar sound was gaining a strong foothold in country music, with players like Brother Oswald in Roy Acuff's band and Jimmie Helms in Hank Williams's group being heavily influenced by the best of the Hawaiian virtuosos. When Jimmie Rodgers, known to many today as the "father of country music," used a dobro guitar player on many of his recordings, that cinched its place in musical history.

Closeup view of a dobro guitar. Many players, like Marty LePore, whose hands we see here, play standing up with a strap over their neck, holding the dobro in this position.

RECYCLING A SLIDE GUITAR OF YOUR OWN

As far as I'm concerned, the world needs more dobro players and slide-guitar players of all sorts. Why don't you try a slide guitar, just for fun? This is how to get started.

Find an old lap guitar — any old guitar, perhaps one that has a warped neck and has become less useful as an ordinary guitar — somewhere in a junk store, basement, garage, or wherever. The warped neck is no problem, since you want the strings to be high off the fret board. In fact, you may need to purchase a nut raiser (the nut is the resting point of the strings — near the end of the neck) or make a higher, flat-topped nut to raise the strings up. (Check your local music store for nut raisers or nut blanks.) Many steel-string guitars have arched fret boards with the strings stretched in an arch over them. You'll want the surface of the string plane to be as flat as possible, so the steel bar will contact all the strings at once.

You'll need to acquire some sort of bar to use for a slide. There are two main types available commercially. One, called a *bullet bar*, is a heavy round steel cylinder, with a rounded end. This type of bar is favored by pedal steel players, but was also used by players like Sol Hoopii, one of the most famous Hawaiian virtuosos. The other type, called a *Stevens bar*, has indentations on each side and on top. Dobro players favor these bars, finding them easier to hang onto for things like hammer-ons and pull-offs (maneuvers not used in pedal steel playing).

Of course if you've got a suitable guitar laying around already, you don't need to head for a music store before you can start trying your hand at steel playing. As I said before, the early players used pocketknives, metal combs, the handles of kitchen knives, and other things. A deep-throat socket (that's part of a tool for working on autos), say around 3/4 to 7/16 inch in diameter, would also work. Generally, a heavier bar works better and gives a better sound—up to a point, of course.

Blues players in the Mississippi delta area picked up the Hawaiian technique and incorporated it into their music, using whatever they could find for a slide. The neck of a long-necked bottle came to be used in playing slide-style while holding the guitar in the normal fashion, and the style became known as *bottleneck guitar*.

While commercially produced glass and steel bottlenecks are available, you can also manufacture your own from a variety of materials. A long-neck bottle with straight sides to the neck is an obvious choice. If you happen to have a bottle-cutter, just cut off the neck. If you don't, there are other ways to get the neck off, such as scoring it with a triangular file where you want it to come off. It should then break there when tapped firmly just below the scored line. You can then grind off sharp edges using the file, but remember to always use goggles when working with glass. Another method is to soak a string in gasoline, tie the string around the neck where you want the bottle cut, and set fire to the string. Let it burn till the glass is good and hot, then plunge the bottle into cold water.

Various kinds of metal tubing, particularly stainless steel or hard brass, also work, and give a different sound from the one you get with glass. And the deep-throat socket that fits your pinkie is a good ready-made choice if you happen to have one. If not, it would be more expensive to buy than a metal slide, but it gives a more solid, hefty sound. (Lowell George, of Little Feat, used one of these in his amazing electric slide work.)

TUNING YOUR SLIDE GUITAR

Now all you need are some tunings to try out. Most dobro players favor an open G tuning that goes like this: G, B, D, G, B, D. These are the same notes you get when you finger a G chord in standard tuning, except for the first (highest) string. This high D note is found at the third fret, second string. Sometimes I finger my G chord using this note. (See G chord fingering in Fig. 16, Section B, in Chapter 4.) Since this is a lower note than usual on the higher string, you may want to use a heavier gauge string there.

A D tuning also arose out of the original slack key system: D, A, D, F-sharp, A, D. In this tuning all but the fourth and fifth strings are lowered, so that again, heavier strings may be called for. The G tuning above was modified from an earlier tuning that went: D, G, D, G, B, D. The two lower strings in this tuning were raised to create a parallel situation between the bottom three and top three strings, a situation that is quite convenient musically. The same thing can be done with this D tuning, which would change it to F-sharp, A, D, F-sharp, A, D. This way you can play the same passage high or low in one position. Very handy.

It was discovered that these original tunings produced a better sound if raised a whole step. The result is an A tuning and an E tuning: E, A, E, A, C-sharp, E; E, B, E, G-sharp, B, E. The former is printed right on the neck of the hollow-neck lap guitar I have, and is apparently a standard tuning used in much of the sheet music available for Hawaiian-guitar. If you should happen to find an old Hawaiian-guitar book in a used-book store or secondhand shop, the opening pages will probably give you the tuning used.

If you want to get just a bit fancier you could try one of these three tunings: E^7: B, D, E, G-sharp, B-sharp, E; C-sharp M^7: E, B, E, G-sharp, C-sharp, E; C^6: C, G, E, A, C, E. In all cases these tunings are listed from the sixth, or lowest, string. These tunings evolved as the steel guitar was used to play more sophisticated music. The latter two tunings are sources of the tunings used on modern pedal steel guitars, which have more strings and have pedals and levers that alter the pitch of notes by altering the string length. In the older style of steel playing—the style you'll be playing unless you have those pedals and levers—these effects are achieved by altering the angle of the bar, or by bending one of the strings with a finger on the hand holding the bar.

Most Hawaiian-guitar players and dobro players finger-pick, using picks on the thumb and two fingers. Some players, notably Tut Taylor, hold the instrument in their lap and flat-pick it. I finger-pick, using three fingers and the thumb, having adapted it from my style of guitar-picking. Whatever works best for you is what you should do.

Unless there is a specific sound you are going for, you should experiment around with the various tunings I've given you and any others you can find or invent. Many players use more than one tuning, either retuning their instrument or experimenting on an extra one. Bear in mind, though, that if you're using an instrument not built for lap-style slide guitar, it's important to notice how much tension you're putting on the instrument when tuning the strings up tight. If the neck is already warped, don't worry about too much tension, but the necks sometimes pull out of the joint, or a bridge can pull off. If you're using a guitar built for steel strings (these have pin bridges or tailpieces), and the instrument is structurally sound with proper string gauging, these problems won't arise.

In bottleneck style, some players fret normally and wear the slide on the little finger, using open or standard tunings. Most of the earlier bottleneck players used the Hawaiian slack-key tunings given above, or similar tunings. In fact the first D tuning I described has become known as "Vestapol" or "Sebastopol" tuning, named for a song for which this tuning was used.

Adjusting the Action on a Fretted Guitar

Whether you have a new guitar or a used one, the factor that affects its playability the most is called *action*. This means, basically, how far do you have to press the strings down to make a clear tone? (This wouldn't apply to lap-style slide playing, but some bottleneck players both fret and use a slide.) You can adjust the action in a variety of ways, provided the neck of the guitar is not warped beyond help. Most better guitars have steel-reinforced adjustable necks that are really quite simple to work, but you should be careful not to tighten the adjusting nut too much or you'll break the rod inside the neck, and then you'll be in trouble. Most often the nut is under a plate on the headstock of the instrument, but occasionally you'll find it inside the body at the heel of the neck. In the latter case, you will do the adjusting through the sound hole using an allen wrench or a nut driver. No more than a quarter-turn should ever be necessary to tighten the nut.

Often you can lower the action by filing down the bridge saddle a bit, and sometimes you can improve the action by cutting the grooves deeper into the nut. Since most of these operations are rather simple, they are usually not too expensive when turned over to someone set up to do them. I would recommend that if you decide to work on your own guitar, you first purchase a repair manual that will tell you what tools you need. The best, though also the most expensive, is Don E. Teeter's *The Acoustic Guitar: Adjustment, Care, Maintenance, and Repair*. (See the *Resources* section on repair manuals for information on how to order the book.)

If you're not sure what adjustments your guitar needs, don't hesitate to ask the opinion of someone who plays well. Guitars come out of the factory with medium action, since not everyone wants low action. Those who play hard (such as bluegrass flat-pickers) usually want the action a bit higher. So if you're looking for very low action, even a brand-new guitar may need a bit of adjustment.

Sometimes action can be improved by changing to a lighter gauge of string or by switching from steel strings to silk-and-steel ones, which produce less tension on the neck when tuned up to pitch. Usually, a guitar that is made for steel strings won't perform well with nylon strings, though there are exceptions to that rule. Never put steel strings on a guitar made for nylon or gut strings, though. Steel-string guitars have pin bridges or tail-pieces, and classic-style guitars (made for nylon or gut) have tie-on bridges.

Collecting a Set of Drums

Guitars, of course, are not the only instruments I've rescued and recycled from unlikely places. My whole family is currently enjoying a set of drums that was put together over a period of time for very little total investment.

It all started with a cymbal a friend was throwing away after he'd traded an old VW body for a new (to him) set of drums. Then came a headless bass drum for free from the local St. Vincent DePaul store. (Someone had purchased a set and left this part because "it lacks something.") Next came a strange snare drum that I purchased for two dollars from the Salvation Army.

About the time I glommed onto the snare, I began to think I might have the makings of a whole drum set, so I started mentioning it to friends. As a result—from two directions at once—I received a headless piccolo snare and a large collection of assorted drum hardware. So I trundled off to the local drum store to see what I needed to round out the set. By making some judicious trades and buying used equipment, I was able to assemble an admittedly funky, but quite enjoyable, trap set consisting of bass, high-hat, snare, tom-tom, bongos (purchased minus one head from a local pawnshop for $5) and three cymbals, all for an actual out-of-pocket cost of around $30.

If that $30 price tag bothers you, watch the newspaper classifieds for used drum sets. The lowest quote I've seen lately is $50 (very rare deal at that), which was for a set that probably needed another $20 or $30 worth of heads and hardware to get it going. I figure that money spent repairing or setting up a used instrument should be compared to what an equivalent ready-to-go instrument would cost if purchased from a music store or pawnshop, or through a newspaper ad. You may also want to compare it to the cost of a used TV or a year's entertainment downtown, since you might well save that much

The interior of Seattle's Folkstore, with proprietor Stu Herrick.

money by entertaining yourself, your family, and your friends with your recycled musical instrument.

Harmonica Recycling

The harmonica is perhaps the most portable of all instruments—other than your voice and hands, of course. The fact that you can carry it with you just about anywhere makes it easier to find time to practice, too. Once you really start to wail, sooner or later you'll blow out your first harp—one hole won't work anymore either on blow or draw, or a note will go flat. This, of course, is part of the dues you pay for soulful playing, but, when it happens, don't throw the harp away: Recondition it instead!

Jim McLaughlin, a good friend of mine, learned how to do this from Cham-ber Hwang (who happens to be head of research for the M. Hohner Company) and—as you'd expect—Hwang's methods really work.

McLaughlin claims that nine times out of ten a "broken" reed is actually just one that is full of grunge (it can happen no matter how careful you've been), or simply in need of being bent further out from the reed plate (if it's a blow note that won't sound) or further in (in the case of a silent draw note). And, even if your harp has actually gone out of tune, you can fix it if your ear is good enough to tell you when it's right again.

Here's Jim's technique for reconditioning mouth harps: First, remove the appropriate cover plate (the top if you need to fix a blow note, or the bottom if a draw note is out of kilter) from your harmonica. If the cover is held in place with screws, just remove the fasteners and lift the plate free. Covers (like the Marine Band's) that are secured with nails can sometimes be pulled off by hand but will usually have to be pried free (don't bend the cover!) with a knife or small screwdriver.

Once the lid is removed, check the "bad" reed for gunk or corrosion. You can clean these deposits from the inside of your harp with a toothpick or small screwdriver, but be careful not to scratch the reeds. While you're at it, you might notice—if you hold your instrument up to the light—small scratches on the reeds that look like they were put there on purpose. If so, don't worry about them. The factory tunes notes that are sharp by making a light scratch across the reed near the point where it is connected to the reed plate to make the thin metal vibrate more slowly. To raise a flat note, on the other hand, the Hohner folks file just a very little material off the end of the reed. If you try this trick, be sure to shove a piece of index card—or some other stiff paper—under the end of the reed to raise it up and to protect other parts that don't need filing. (Jim suggests that you use a knife file for this delicate work.)

If a reed is bent too close to the reed plate, this malformation can cause the note to hesitate or not come at all. To correct the problem, just bend the reed lightly away from the plate if it's a blow note that won't come, or a bit in if it's a draw note. The harp will still play with the cover off, so you can try it out if you're careful not to get your lips or mustache in the way of the reeds.

To put the cover back on, just replace the nails or screws that you removed. Jim warns that the nails will sometimes become too loose to keep the piece in place. When this happens, he uses tape to hold his harp together. (Other alternatives would be small screws, thumbtacks, rubber bands, or small metal stove bolts.)

Of course, it's possible that a reed in your harmonica is actually broken. If so, hang onto the instrument anyway. The reed can be replaced, or you can save the good reeds to fix broken ones in another harp. You can easily pry the reeds from the rivet that holds them, and slip replacements over the rivet, tapping them gently into place with a hammer.

As with other used instruments, there is a point of diminishing returns on harp recycling. You may be able to extend the life of your harmonica by using these techniques, though: You should hit the instrument against the palm of your hand or your leg when you're done playing to knock out residual moisture. And remember not to eat or drink while playing—fruit juice and other such things help to corrode the reeds and shorten the life of your harmonica. Preventative techniques do as much as anything to make a harmonica last longer.

Finding Bargains in Working Condition

If refurbishing instruments scares you, nothing says you *have* to start your down-home music pickin' and grinnin' with a piece of equipment that you found in a barn somewhere. But you don't have to pay full list price for an instrument in good working condition, either.

There are many ways to buy musical instruments without paying an arm and a leg for them. Ever since the Beatles rocketed to stardom, carrying the guitar with them,

An array of inexpensive guitars in a Goodwill store.

production figures on guitars have skyrocketed. One result of the sheer numbers of guitars being made is that the market value on medium-quality used guitars has gone down as the availability has gone up. You can now often find a real good used guitar (usually Japanese-made) for just over $100. A more patient and diligent search might turn up a better deal yet. Truly decent older American-made guitars such as Kay or Harmony have been found for as little as $5 this way.

Usually these better deals will require some fixing up to make them really playable, but quite often that means nothing more than a new set of strings. So haunt garage sales and swap meets. Check out secondhand stores in your area. Read the newspaper classified ads and run an ad of your own. And above all, be patient. Just keep on looking until you find the deal you want.

If you don't know how to tell whether an instrument is playable and worth the price being asked, take someone along who does know. And don't be afraid to bargain a little on asking price. Bargaining will help you in two ways: (1) It'll sometimes cut the cost of the good instruments you buy, and (2) if you ever find yourself stuck with a piece of equipment that looked good but turned out to be worthless except as a decoration, you won't mind taking your loss and hanging it on the wall, if you didn't pay much for it in the first place.

Remember, too, that it doesn't always take money to "buy" something you want. I once traded a '48 GMC pickup truck for an old electric guitar, a microphone, three instrument speakers (now in a P.A. system), a transducer-type acoustic-guitar pickup and pre-amp, and a phase shifter (an electronic device that makes an electric guitar sound something like an electric organ with revolving speakers). I then swapped a beautiful old railroad coal stove to a music store for an amplifier, some wire, and a couple more speakers—and, presto—I was in the entertainment business with a sound reinforcement system.

Of course, my trades didn't stop there. I've since swapped a story about the deal I just described to *The Mother Earth News* for a year's subscription. And, recently, I traded the electric guitar (after doing some work on it) for a reel-to-reel tape recorder, and bartered an old fiddle for another set of drums, which I've used to upgrade and add to the $30 set I described earlier.

In short, the possibilities for finding musical instruments and being given them absolutely free, for purchasing such equipment at very low cost, and for trading for guitars, drums, microphones, amps, or anything you can think of, are truly endless. Look around, ask around, advertise (not necessarily just in the newspapers). You'll be surprised at what you can turn up when people know you're in the market for a donation, a good buy, or an interesting swap.

Learning to Play the Guitar

I NEVER took guitar lessons, but I'm sure I could have learned faster if I had found someone who knew the licks I wanted to know and asked him to teach them to me. I've learned through trial and error, and although I developed my own style by never learning anyone else's, I think I went the long way around. Occasionally, a sage remark from an experienced player filtered its way gradually into my consciousness. For instance:

"Look for the melody notes as you pick and strum. One by one you'll find them and pretty soon you'll be picking out the melodies while you're picking and strumming." —Dale Hustler.

"Sleep on it. Your brain-to-hand coordination develops partly through practice and partly through the passage of time."—Many musicians have said this.

"Finger-picking patterns are OK to get started on, but ultimately you want to use your fingers for whatever notes you want to play. At some point the patterns only get in the way."—Dale Hustler.

If you are looking for a teacher, I would say that the first step is to figure out exactly what you want to learn. Do you want to play like Doc Watson or Chet Atkins or Mississippi John Hurt or Bonnie Rait or somebody else? If you can focus on the style you want to learn, it will be easier to find a teacher who can lead you where you want to go (or at least avoid one who can't). If you hear a player doing something you'd like to do, it doesn't hurt to ask questions, and if you have a lot of questions, offer to pay the person for the time it takes to answer them. This same musician might be willing to give you lessons.

Around where I live, weekly lessons available from music stores cost about $7.50 per half hour, payable a month at a time in advance. The trouble with this type of program is that it doesn't always fit the individual's learning rhythm. Perhaps you'd do better with an hour lesson once a month. Books with accompanying records (look under mail-order houses in the *Resources* section) would allow you to set your own pace. This method of learning would cost about the same as one or two lessons at a store, and if it works for you, you'd probably get more for your money than from a private teacher. But some folks need to have someone watch what they are doing at the beginning and give them pointers.

Even though I've been playing the guitar pretty steady for the last 17 years, I certainly don't know everything there is to know about pickin'—not close to half—but I have learned a trick or two that I'd like to pass along with the understanding that there are lots more ways to go about it than my way.

Getting Started

If you are a beginner, the hardest part of learning to play the guitar is making your fingers learn the chord patterns, and the second-hardest part is getting callouses built up so you can stand to press those strings down long enough to play more than a song or two. All I can tell you is hang in there. Learn at least a couple of chords and some songs you can use them on. Instead of "practicing," just play your songs and concentrate on the music; it'll take your mind off the pain. If you stick with it, in a short while your hands will start getting used to playing, and you'll be over the hump. Once your fingers get the idea of pressing on strings and changing from one fingering to another, it becomes much easier to learn new chords.

That's what you want to do next—learn more chords and songs with more complicated arrangements. There's a wide variety of books on the market with diagrams of chords, some with pictures of a hand playing them. If you want to progress with reasonable speed, one of these books is indispensable at the beginning. You can find one at nearly any music store, or order one by mail from one of the sources listed in the *Resources* section. (Some chord diagrams are also included in this chapter—see Figs. 9 and 11.)

Chord Progression

As you move along, you will notice that most American folk songs and most popular songs are built around three chords. Of course there is wide variation, and many songs contain four- or five-chord progressions, but the main part of most of these songs consists of a tonic, a subdominant, and a dominant chord.

Those are pretty big words, so I'll give some examples: In the key of C, the tonic chord is C, the subdominant is F, and the dominant is G. In the key of E, these chords are E, A, and B (which have the same mathematical relationship as the chords in the key of C). In G, the chords are G, C, and D; and in D, D, G, and A. There you have the four most popular keys guitarists play in. If you learn seven chords, you can play three-chord songs in all four keys and throw in A to boot! (A's chords are A, D, and E.) Now, if you learn minor and seventh variations on these chords, you can fake your way through just about anything from Christmas carols to ragtime jug-band blues.

Once you understand the idea of chord progression, you can start *transposing*. That means playing a song in a different key from the one you know it in. Transposing comes in handy if you come across a song written in a key you can't sing in, or if you play a song you already know with someone who does it in a different key. When you really get into it, you may find it easier to think of chord progressions by numbers rather than keynotes. The number system is particularly useful when you learn all the chords up the neck and you are playing mostly in barre positions.

A three-chord song is called a 1-4-5 if that is the order the chords are played in. The tonic chord is No. 1, being the note on the diatonic scale the key is named for; the subdominant is No. 4 because it is named for the fourth note on the scale from No. 1; the dominant is No. 5. A three-chord song could also progress in a 1-5-4 pattern, in a 1-4-1-5 one, or in many more complex arrangements of the same three chords. Sometimes folks will use the term 1-4-5 to mean "a three-chord song," regardless of the order in which the chords are arranged, but ordinarily, when musicians use these numbers when speaking to each other, they mean that the chords occur in that order. The number system is a quick way of describing the chord progression of a particular song.

While you're making chords with one hand, what is the other hand doing? It's either strumming, pick-strumming, flat-picking, or finger-picking. I've see some players use a combination of all four. Most people start out either strumming a rhythm or finger-picking a particular rhythmic pattern, and gradually get fancier.

Tablature

In order to learn different pick-strum patterns and finger-picking patterns, it's useful to know how to read a style of guitar notation called *tablature*, which often has the standard musical notation written directly above it. Tablature is a more graphic way than standard notation of showing how to play something on the guitar. The system uses a six-line staff, each line of which represents a string on the guitar, as you view the instrument looking down on it. If a 3 appears on the fifth line, this means that the fifth string should be played while fingered at the third fret (see Fig. 6).

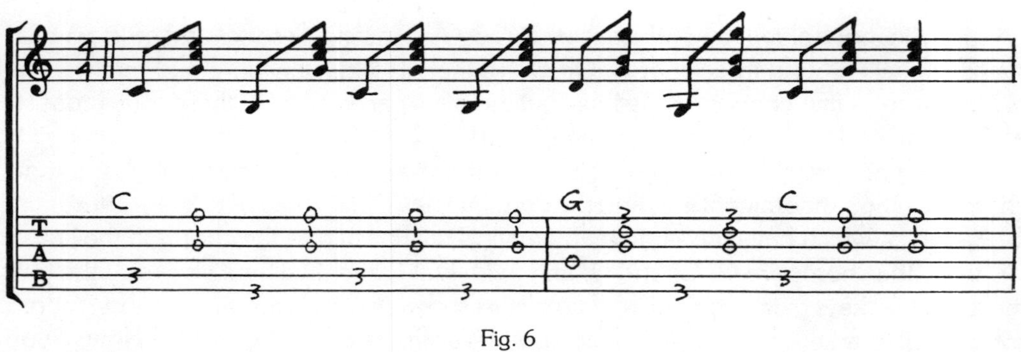

Fig. 6

The direction of a pick stroke is indicated above the staff by a v (upstroke) or a ⊓ (downstroke) (see Fig. 7). Sometimes the letter for the chord is written above the staff. Letters within the staff call for such tricks as slides (s), pull-offs (p), and hammer-ons (h).

To do a *slide*, you play a fretted note and keep the pressure on it while you slide your fretting finger up the string to another fret, so that the first note slides into a higher note. To do a *pull-off*, you play a fretted note, then remove your fretting finger fast enough that the open note or a note you are fretting below the original note will ring out. A *hammer-on* is

Fig. 7

the opposite of a pull-off. You play a note, then bring your finger down on a higher note fast enough that the note still rings out. Sometimes, particularly on an electric guitar, a player will create notes just by hammering-on with no need for plucking the string. You might hear a rapid combination of hammer-ons and pull-offs with the hammer-on creating the string vibration.

A *bent note* is used mostly in the blues style. The note is bent by literally bending the string to the side while you fret and pluck a note. Players like B.B. King, who play electric guitars with slinky strings, will often bend a note through as much as two whole steps, the equivalent of four frets' distance on the neck! On an acoustic guitar with lighter gauge strings, you might hold a bent note for one whole step.

No system of notation is as good as hearing a song played for giving you an idea of how it's supposed to sound, but much of the tablature in print is transcribed from recorded work. Standard notation is used with tablature to indicate the duration of notes, though satisfactory methods have been devised for including that in the tab notation too. Fig. 6 is a simple pick-strum pattern, and Fig. 7 is a slightly more complex version of the same thing.

You can use this sort of alternating bass note strumming pattern for a wide variety of country and folk tunes, and eventually move out of it into the melody flat-picking style made famous by Maybelle Carter. In that style the melody grows out of the alternating bass note lines, but the pick-strum pattern also continues to give a bass-rhythm-melody arrangement. The bass notes I've shown in Figs. 6 and 7 for the chords C and G are not the only possible ones. For whatever chord you're playing, you should pick out the bass notes you like, and maybe alternate a couple of patterns.

Where I've indicated the strumming of three strings at a time, it's not mandatory that you hit only those three. Since you're fingering the whole chord, it's fine if you hit four or more. Speaking of fingering the whole chord, a lot of beginners learn that C chord without using the little finger at the third fret on the fifth string. I advise you to get your little finger into the act as soon as possible. Why let one finger be lazy and diminish your ability to play notes by 20 to 25 percent? (The percentage depends upon whether or not you use your thumb. I favor using the thumb because there's a hammer-on lick in the F chord used in country music that can't be done without using the thumb for the bass note rather than barring the chord.) Anyway, I use the little finger in the C chord and again in the G at the third fret on the first string (the first string is the highest pitch; the sixth is the lowest). I feel that this fingering makes it easier to change between the two chords, since it requires less movement of the hand.

In Fig. 7 I've added a short upstroke after the strumming of the chord. Although I've marked just the first string, it's OK if you hit two or three. The effect is the same: You get a kind of "chicken pickin'," or country-shuffle. It adds a lot of bounce to the song. Another way to get this effect is to chop off the notes of the strum by deadening the strings just after strumming them. You do this by lifting your fingers off the fret board a bit, but not off the strings.

To get the full effect of this second style, you have to chop off the upstroke note and the chord itself a bit. This means cutting the notes short rather than letting them ring. One way I do this is to use the palm of my pick hand to deaden the strings just after (or sometimes while) I pluck them. You have to play awhile to master this technique, so if you're just getting started, don't let yourself get too frustrated trying to figure out how it works.

When you play chords up the neck, or play any chord without open strings (meaning you're fretting all the notes in the chord), it's much easier to chop off the notes wherever you want by just lifting your fingers a bit. In order to get the feel of this style, you might try it on some barre chords first.

All the strokes in Fig. 6 are downstrokes. In Fig. 7, I've added some upstrokes.

Just as there are a lot of ways to approach playing the guitar, there are also a variety of ways for writing tablature, using different symbols. In most cases the method is explained at the beginning of whatever book you are learning from. Much of what I've said here is also applicable to playing other stringed, fretted instruments, such as the banjo, mandolin, and dulcimer.

Tuning the Guitar

One of the first things you need to know is how to tune your instrument. When it is not in tune, you won't get as much pleasure out of playing it, whether you realize this consciously or not. Harmonious vibrations make you feel good, and dissonant ones have the opposite effect. Guitars can be tuned to themselves when you don't have a piano, tuning fork, or other fixed-note device. Any guitar book for beginners explains how to tune by this method, the main trick being to train your ear to hear when two notes are exactly the same. What you're listening for is a beat frequency, a particular throbbing of the tone. When the throbbing or pulsating sound ceases, the string you are tuning will be in tune with the other strings, or other note you're tuning it to.*

I use three or four methods to check the tuning on my guitar, including the fifth-fret/fourth-fret method most books show. I also check all strings against the G string, and go for

* A musical note is created by something (a guitar string, vocal chord, and so on) vibrating rhythmically. The frequency of that vibration determines the pitch of the note. When two notes are in harmony, their frequencies bear a mathematical relationship to each other. For instance, with two notes an octave apart, the higher one vibrates exactly twice as often as the lower one. The vibrations, then, reinforce each other. Picture a couple of drummers playing together. If they are all keeping the same time, they create a powerful rhythm. Sometimes they'll all be hitting drums on the same beat. If they are all playing a different rhythm (never hitting the same beats), it's just irritating noise. Any two or more notes in harmony are like the drummers playing together. When your guitar or piano is out of tune, or when any two notes are not harmonious (discordant), it's like the drummers playing different rhythms that don't fit together. You don't perceive the individual vibrations, but you feel the dissonance, and it makes you uncomfortable.

a seventh-fret/ eighth-fret check, which is similar to the standard method, except that the higher string is fretted to gain a note an octave higher.

The quality of your guitar has a definite effect on your ability to tune it well. Some guitars can benefit from the fitting of better tuning machines, with a higher gear ratio and smoother action. If you don't know whether your own guitar is extra difficult to tune, consult an experienced player and have him try it. When your strings are worn out, it eventually becomes impossible to tune them and make them sound good together. If you don't live near a music store, you can purchase new strings by mail from any of the mail-order houses in the *Resources* section.

On most arch-top guitars the bridge isn't glued down. If the bridge gets out of place, the guitar will not play in tune, particularly up the neck. If you have one of these, you can check to see whether your bridge placement is correct by playing a note at the 12th fret and then making a harmonic note by placing your finger lightly on the string just above the fret and picking it with your other hand. You may have to move the fretting finger up and down a bit to find just the right spot, especially if the bridge is off. What you're listening for are beat frequencies. If you don't hear them, the notes are in tune. You need to check all six strings. On most good electric guitars the position of the bridge saddle is adjustable for each string.

Identifying Chord Changes

Players who have perfect pitch and those who have been playing for many years can often identify chords just by the sound. If you can't do this, it certainly is no breach of etiquette to ask what key a tune is being played in at a jam session. It is also appropriate to position yourself where you can see another guitar player's hand in order to pick up on chord changes.

After you know enough songs and have been playing for a while, you will get to the point where you'll recognize chord changes in most songs. You still may need to be told the key (even the pros yell out the key before they start a song on jam night at the local saloon), but you'll know when the group is moving from C to F or G.

A Pattern for Lead Breaks

A lead break is a guitar solo, say, between verses of a song. Generally, a lead break for a given song is based on the same scale of notes used for the melody. Take a given song and find the notes being used in the melody, near the position where you are fingering the chord. You'll discover that there is a particular scale being used, with some notes being played together with one chord, some with another, and some notes always used.

I was once shown a pattern of notes for a particular key that would make picking up a Doc Watson riff easier. My friend Jeff Smith called it a "blues pattern" and explained that one could improvise blues breaks using these notes in the key of E. He said the same pattern could be used for a boogie-woogie break in G. I've been using it for years now and have discovered that playing this pattern in the blues position in the key for the boogie version can give a different, blusier, feel to the break.

Fig. 8 shows this pattern in the key of E. The pattern can be easily transposed to another key by moving the starting point to whatever fret gives you the name note of the desired key on the first (and sixth) string. If you transpose it to the key of A, you'll start the pattern as though the fifth fret were the nut, using all the notes at that fret. Below that point, between the fifth fret and the nut, you'll use the same pattern as on the five-fret space below the 12th fret. In any case, the whole pattern is repeated above the 12th fret.

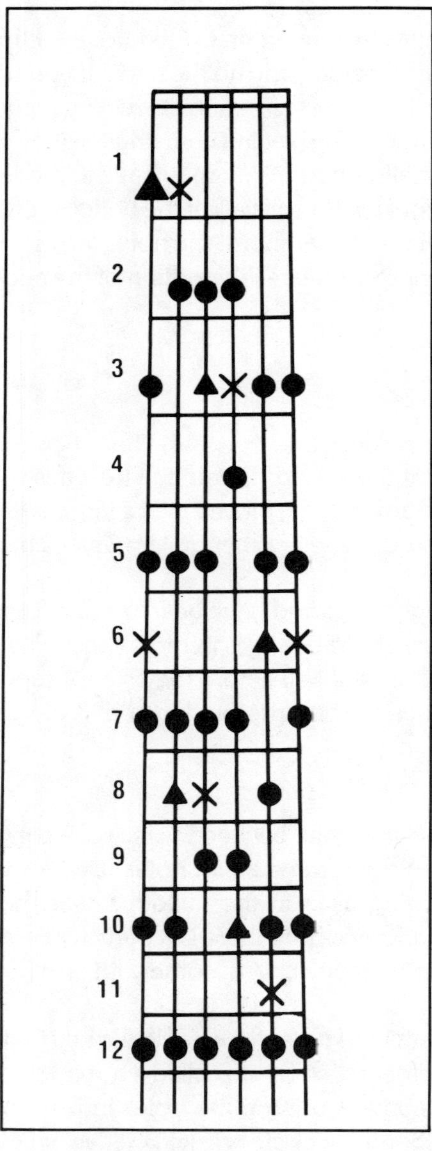

Fig. 8. A blues pattern in E minor or G.

Some notes in the diagram are indicated by an X and others by a triangle. I call these *transitional* or *blue* notes. I use the X notes frequently in improvising lead lines for city-style (Chicago) blues in E. I use the same note in the key of G for more of a country or country-blues feel. This pattern in the key of E is related to the E-minor scale. The X notes are the flatted seventh in the E diatonic scale. You'll find those seventh chords in the blues a lot. The triangle notes are the flatted seventh in the G diatonic scale. Those notes are used for playing boogie breaks and walking bass lines in G.

There are also other transitional notes you can use, as well as other techniques such as shifting modes, which means playing a different scale for the same key. For example, if you play a "do-re-mi" scale along one string on your guitar, you'll notice that some of the notes are two frets apart, while others are only one fret apart. If you change the arrangement of those intervals, you're changing the mode.

The pattern in Fig. 8 shows you why E minor is known as the *relative minor* of G. The E-minor scale is the same as the G-major scale, except that the *tonic note*—the starting point—is different. Every major scale has a relative minor. On the guitar you find the name note for the relative minor key three frets below the name note of the major key. So, for example, if you wanted to play a country-blues lead in the key of E, the pattern in Fig. 8 would start on the ninth fret. D-flat (also known as C-sharp) is the relative minor for the key of E. You'll find a relative minor chord in many a chord progression, too.

Chord Diagrams

Fig. 9 shows most of the chord forms I use. Most of them are shown at the open, or first, position, and where you can use hammer-on or pull-off notes, I have put a little circle above a string that has a fret position shown (meaning that it can be played open), or put an X on a fret position above a dot. (There are also other possibilities I haven't shown—you should experiment.)

I use my little finger to fret chords, and I want to encourage you to gain control over yours and use it. In some of these chord fingerings I will indicate with an X above the string where you could deaden rather than play an indicated fretted note. An X above a string with no other indication means the string is not played or deadened. I also use my thumb for fingering bass notes on the lower two strings. In some barre forms, this method becomes an alternative; using the thumb allows you one important hammer-on note that wouldn't be available in the barre form.

When a chord form is movable, you can play it anywhere up and down the neck. Of course it becomes a different chord in each position, based on the keynote, which is marked in each movable form by a circle around the dot showing the fretted note or open note that is the key of the chord, the note the chord is named for. If you want to use the movable form for a chord other than the one shown, simply find the keynote on the same string my version has that note on, and play the chord at that position. How do you find that note? Fig. 10 shows the note names at each fret position up to the 12th fret. The whole thing repeats starting at that point. Any three-note or even two-note chord is also movable, of course (see Fig. 16, Section B). The possibilities are nearly endless!

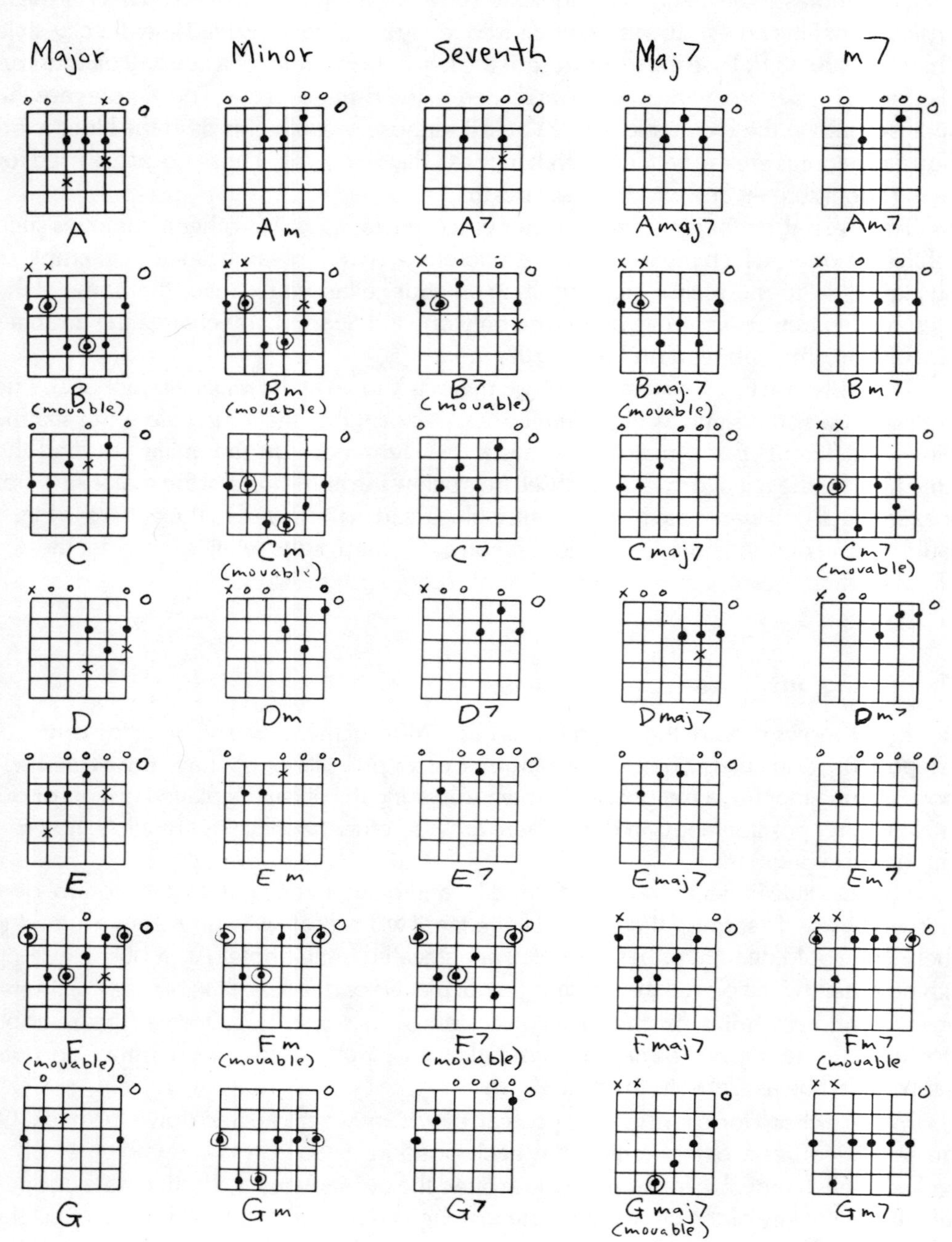

Fig. 9. These diagrams all start at the nut, or "zero fret" as indicated by the number on the right. Were the chords being fingered further up the neck, a fret number would be indicated.

Fig. 10. Guitar fingerboard chart.

A *diminished* chord (written with a minus sign), by the way, can be named for either of the notes in the chord—in other words, for one of four notes. The diminished chord in Fig. 11 could also be E-flat, A, or F-sharp/G-flat. This means that there are actually only four different diminished chords in the 12-note scale, though there are three different inversions of the chord per octave, depending on which note is on top, which is in the middle, and which is the lowest, or bass, note in the chord. An *augmented* chord (written with a plus sign) can be named for one of three different notes, as one note is represented twice. Two notes an octave apart have the same name; the augmented chord contains two such notes. The augmented chord in Fig. 11 could also be A + or C – sharp/D-flat + .

Fig. 11 shows some alternative fingerings I use frequently, as well as some of the jazz chords I use—sixths and ninths, diminished and augmented.

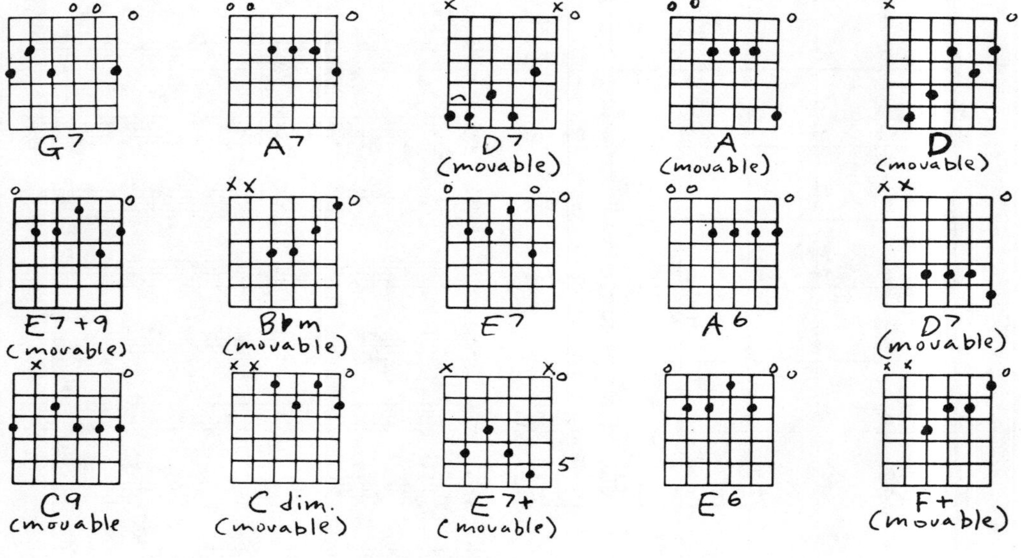

Fig. 11

There are a great many more possibilities. These are just the ones *I* use most often. For more information on chord fingering and chord-progression theory, you should get a good book on the subject (see the *Resources* section).

Intros

Figs. 12 through 16 are intros, or breaks, for guitar, written in both tablature and standard musical notation. These songs are all available on record. Notes linked by a crescent-shaped line with a letter overhead are either slides (s), hammer-ons (h), or pull-offs (p). (See *Tablature*, earlier in this chapter.)

PICK-STRUM PATTERNS

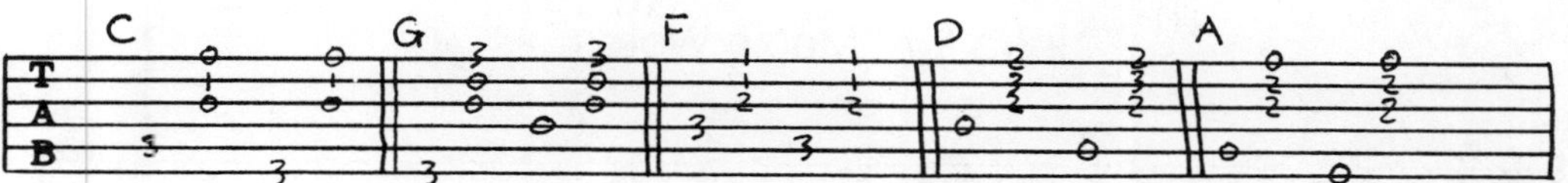

Fig. 12. What we have here are examples of basic pick-strum patterns with an alternating bass note. You don't have to use the bass notes shown here; I just want you to get the idea. These measures are not meant to be played all together, but you can use the elements to play songs in C, G, or D, and apply the idea to other keys as well. As you'll see in the next piece (an intro for "Cabin in the Woods"), I don't always use the same bass notes, and my melody grows out of this alternating bass line.

Intro for "Cabin in the Woods"

Intro for "Magic Words"

Fig. 13. Here's a short intro for "Magic Words," to give you an idea how to play rhythm in three-quarter (waltz) time, and another for "Leave Your Cares Behind," to show what you might do in the key of G in a similar style. I encourage you to take these ideas and develop your own style rather than try to play the way I do. Sometimes it's really frustrating to try to imitate another person's rhythm when your feel for it is different.

Intro for "Leave Your Cares Behind"

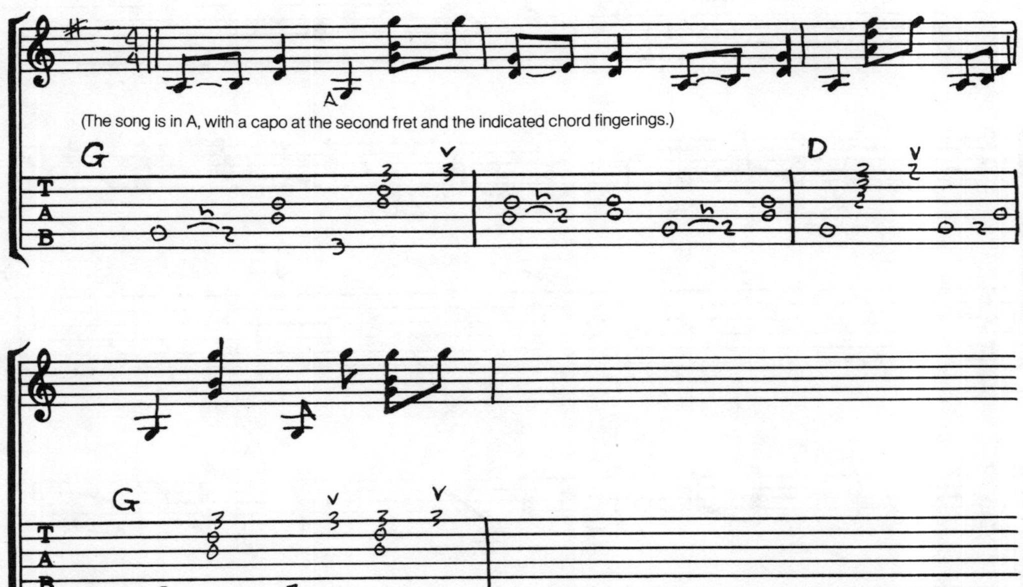

Rhythm Guitar for "Goin' Down to the River"

Fig. 14. This is a slow-rocking blues shuffle in G. Since it's a 12-bar blues, you'll repeat the two-measure G part, go into the C part, repeat the G part again, and after the D/C part do a measure of G and a measure of D. You can speed it up to rock-and-roll. I play this sort of thing in G, C, D, A, and E — open position. While I've indicated mostly single-note parts here, you can hit two or three strings at a time, particularly while you're singing. I've used a down-stroke mark (П) above the staff to indicate a spot where you *don't* hit the string, but the stroke is there to maintain the rhythm.

In the G part, you get the fourth-string, second-fret note simply by moving your finger over from the fifth string. I use my little finger on the first string for the G chord because it's easier to change to C that way. In the C part, you're doing the same thing, just moving the finger over one string. In the D part, you use the little finger to get the third-string, fourth-fret note.

Guitar Part for "My Lady"

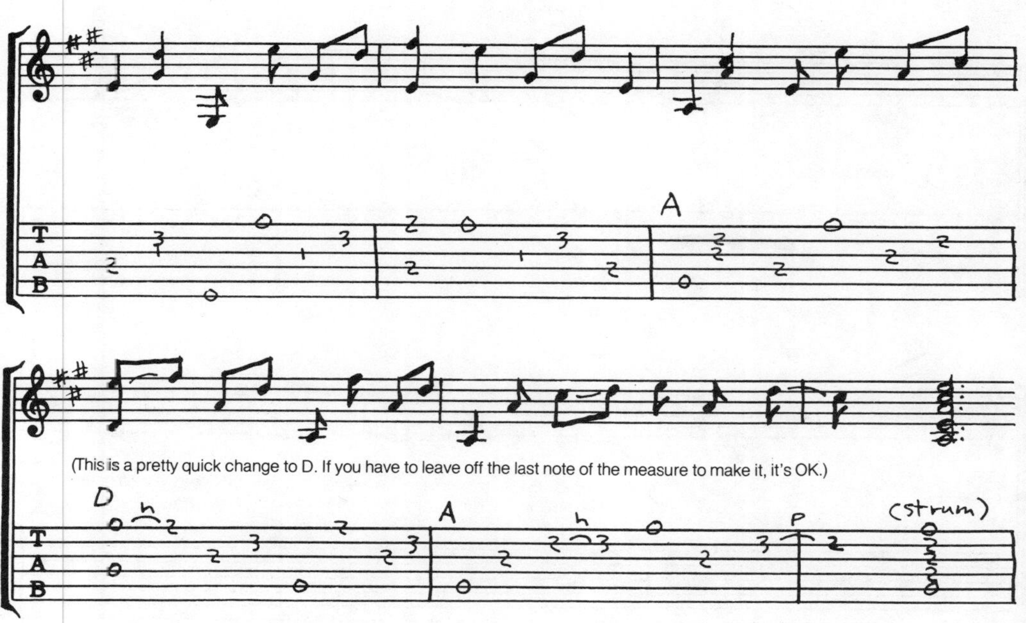

Fig. 15. My finger-picking style may not be unique, but I haven't heard anyone else's that sounds quite like it. I use my thumb and three fingers, where most finger-style players use only two fingers or one finger and the thumb. A notable exception is Chet Atkins. While there are a couple of variations on a basic underlying pattern to my playing, I never just play the pattern for more than a measure or two at a time. You could take any given measure (or two-measure series) from the following piece (which is more than just an intro — it goes through the whole progression) and use it as the basis for whatever notes you want in whatever order. In this finger style the melody can grow out of either part (the alternating bass part or the rhythm part), depending on the key you're playing in. I like D because I can do melodies on the higher strings. In G the melodies come out of the bass. In C they can cross back and forth.

The thumb takes the lower three strings, and the three fingers take one each of the higher strings. Sometimes the index finger is actually playing part of the alternating bass line in what will sound something like *double thumbing,* a style where there is a bass note on every beat.

When I finger my A chord (in the first position) and E chord, I use the end of one finger to fret two strings at once. That means I get the second-fret notes on the second and third strings in A with my middle finger, and the second-fret notes on the fourth and fifth strings in the E chord with the same finger. Depending on the width of your guitar neck and the width of the end of your finger, you may be able to do this fingering, too.

The next piece is similar to this one, though written in the key of D. For this reason and to conserve space, I'm not going to lay the whole thing out. I'll just give the parts containing new tricks or techniques — in particular the chords you slide up the neck and some pull-offs that start way up the neck.

"Mountain Lullaby"

SECTION B

Fig. 16. This is the last half of section B of the tune. The first half is the same except that you don't do the pull-off in the last measure, but play the A chord (F form, fifth fret) straight.

In the first measure of section B you slide the entire form (shown as D) up from two frets below, then slide it all the way up to the indicated fret in the third measure. Although you're only plucking one string, the other fretted notes will ring out some because of the friction of your fingers bumping over the frets. You're doing the same with the D form in section D.

CHORDS FOR SECTIONS A and C

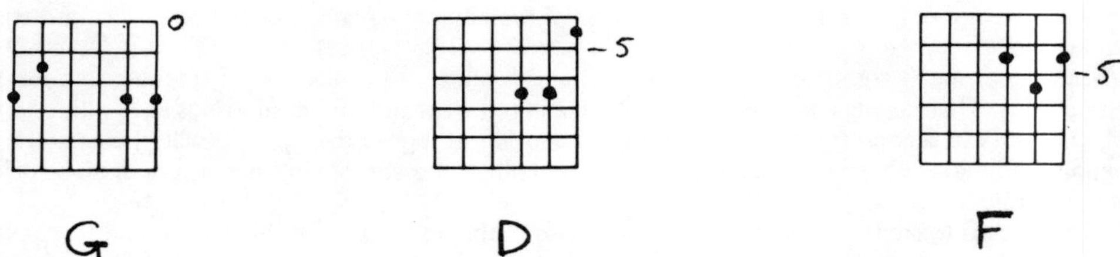

Sections A and C of "Mountain Lullaby" are fairly ordinary parts featuring hammer-ons and pull-offs on the D, G, and A7 chords. The only slightly unusual thing is the G-chord fingering with the D note (third fret, second string), but lots of people use that. You can find the chord-fingering in the guitar chord chart below. I'm also including the movable chord form used for the D and G chords in section B above, and the D form used in section D below.

SECTION D

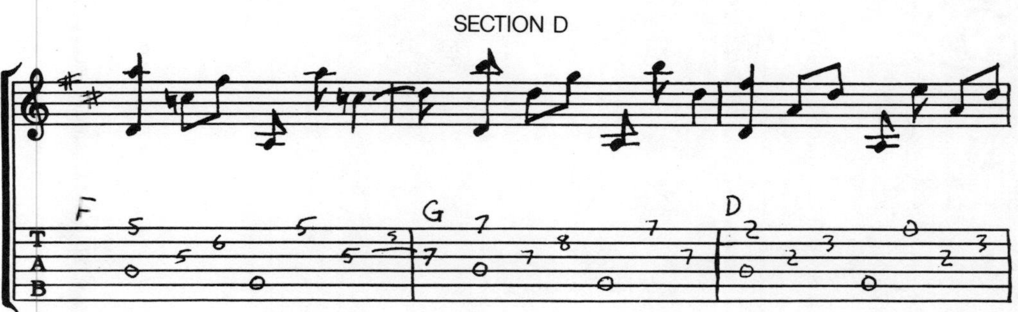

There's another measure of D (making four measures altogether) and then this is repeated for the first half of the D section. In the next half, the first measure below is used, with a measure of D in the first, or open, position to end it the first time, then as follows here to end the piece.

The B section ends with a couple of measures of D, open position.

5

Jamming and Song-Swapping

HAVE you ever gone to a concert and noticed how much fun the performers seemed to be having? Well, you could be having that kind of fun yourself, in your own living room, for free! Just start making your own music—with your friends—instead of shelling out good money to listen to someone else having all the fun.

Do-it-yourself entertainment is much the same as building a house yourself, growing a garden yourself, or doing anything else yourself: It's simply more satisfying when you do it with your own two hands than when you pay someone else to do it for you.

There are other benefits from holding a down-home jam session in your front room or out on the porch, too:

1. As I've already mentioned, you'll be saving money;

2. You'll be building priceless relationships with interesting folks right there in your own neighborhood; and

3. You won't need to hire a babysitter or otherwise worry about what to do with the children. Just sing them to sleep and then knock yourself out on a few of your favorite tunes!

Hoots Can Happen Anywhere, Anytime, with Anybody

Of course, there's no law that says you have to wait for your regular evening social get-togethers if you want to have a music-making session. Not if you have a family. Remember: A jam session is nothing but two or more people (*any* two people) getting together for the purpose of playing music. Any kind of music.

My son and I started singing together when he was only 1½ years old. He was riding on the back of my bicycle as I pedaled up the mountain road we lived on, and he joined in on "A Bicycle Built For Two" (which I was singing as I watched the daisies and other wildflowers we passed wave musically in the breeze).

Since then, my boy has taken up playing the jug. (There's a rude-noises stage that youngsters go through that makes it especially easy to introduce them to jug playing.) He also likes shakers and percussion instruments and, now that he's four, he and his friends are generally thrilled when I set up the drums and then strum something on the guitar for them to drum along with.

And I'm thrilled when my son comes home from preschool singing a new song that he's learned in just one day. It means that he really likes music and he really likes that tune, which will probably get added to our repertoire of "riding-in-the-car" songs. And if you didn't already know it, there are songs for riding in a car, walking, hoeing, pedaling, rowing, pushing, pulling, laughing, crying, lying in the shade, and Lord-knows-what-all! There's a song, or several, for almost any activity. Use them! Make up your own!

But back to excuses for gathering your friends and neighbors together for a little pickin' and grinnin'. You don't really need an excuse the first time or two you want to throw one of these shindigs. Just hang your playin' and singin' onto one end or another—or both—of a few potluck dinners.

"Bring-a-dish" suppers are so easy to stew down into a musical jam. In the first place, the cooks in the crowd get to show off their talents, too, which guarantees satisfaction on several levels. And in the second place, the conversation at such events usually takes on the valuable aspects of a community newsletter.

Need manure for your garden? Looking for a good used truck? Have you got your eyes peeled for some baby clothes for that little one you're expecting? Or do you have manure, a used truck, or baby clothes that you're trying to get rid of? A potluck dinner/musical jam fest is the place for buyers and sellers and swappers of good will to get together and strike their bargains.

The whole idea is just getting together and enjoying each other's company and benefiting from the experience. And nothing draws people together faster or better than a little homegrown music. Heaven on earth already exists, if you know how to open your eyes to it!

Bring All Your Instruments

OK, I've got you convinced. You're ready to have a hoedown, a hootenanny, a musical get-together, a jam session—whatever you want to call it—at your place or in someone else's home. Here's a little tip: If you want that evening to be a real ripsnorter, take all your instruments to the get-together.

In the first place, it'll make the hoot a whole lot more valuable for you and your musical development. By switching off from one instrument to another as the evening goes on (or sometimes during a single song), you'll quickly pick up different points of view about musical arrangement. That is, once you've tried several different parts, you'll find it easier to keep the way they all fit together in mind while you're later playing any one part.

If you usually play lead guitar, try switching off to washtub bass or a set of bongo drums or the spoons or a mandolin or any one of a dozen other instruments for a few numbers. Who knows? You may uncover a hidden talent. At the very least, you're sure to increase your awareness of the whole sound picture your group is painting.

And here's an illustration of another reason you and everyone else should bring more than one instrument to your jam sessions: I've seen a few hoots that more or less resembled a congregation of gunfighters at the local saloon, when six or eight people showed up, each toting a single guitar case and each secretly wondering how she or he might manage to dominate the session or maybe even just squeeze one favorite song in edgewise during the coming confrontation.

That's why I took up playing the washboard, mandolin, banjo, bongos, pocket change, and washtub bass. Not only do I find the music at one of our pickup sessions more pleasing when a percussion instrument (or anything that has a different tonal range from a guitar) is added to the blend, but I also avoid the sinking feeling one gets wondering whether there's really room for yet another guitar in a six-guitar band.

The problems of competition and redundancy of sound need never arise if everyone who arrives brings along an extra instrument or two or three. And if they all do, you'll reap another bonus too: There'll always be something handy for the musicians who drop in unexpectedly, or the folks who've never tried to make music before, to pick up and play. You'll be surprised at the amount of entertainment, satisfaction, and downright *fun* such unexpected additions can add to your hoedown.

And don't overlook the instruments you've brought without maybe even knowing you were bringing them. Things like change and keys, for instance. Loose change in one pocket and a handful of keys in another make an ideal instrument that you can play and dance with at the same time. I don't remember whether I discovered this fact while listening to the radio or as I was watching a group of street musicians, but I do know it works. And if you're as compulsive a player of music as I am, that's a good bit of knowledge to have.

Of course you can put on a pickup jam session without any "real" instruments at all, if you're not too proud to bang on pots, pan lids, jars, or water glasses (you can tune the last two, you know, by varying the amount of water you put in them). One night a bunch of us held just such a hoot out on the porch after a long, hot, summer day. We never did find out what the neighbors thought about the whole affair, but we sure did have a good time! On another occasion, a friend of mine, faced with the prospect of sitting through an evening-long session without his drums, manufactured a whole set of percussion instruments out of what was left of the dinner dishes, and so astounded everyone at the hoot that it soon became a one-man concert!

The Golden Rule at Jam Sessions

And that's the way it should be. Everyone at a hoot should be encouraged to participate in his or her own way and the texture of such get-togethers should change and ebb and flow as their participants learn new instruments, experiment with different ideas in music, pick up new songs, originate new tunes, and otherwise express themselves musically.

So hang loose. Make sure that no one person or group of people always dominates the festivities. Give everyone a chance to join in. Sure, it'll probably be up to a few experienced players (at least in the beginning) to get the ball rolling. But those old hands should go out of their way to pass their instruments around ("Here, *you* play this") or at the very least, let others start some of the tunes. Pretty soon everybody will catch the spirit and start contributing something, maybe even writing a whole new song.

That's a sign that your hoedown is really cookin', and if you're one of the better musicians at the fest, perhaps you should start laying back a little and just holding down the rhythm. Or playing fills and breaks. Or adding a harmony vocal. There's no need for you to do whole arrangements on guitar, voice, and harmonica when everyone in the group is joining in. Relax. Enjoy what others are doing. There's a real high there for everyone when you all tune in on the same vibrations.

That's How You Learn!

And there's something else in it for you, too, when you don't take over the whole show: While you're having all that good, honest, *real* fun, you'll also be increasing your musical awareness and expertise in a number of ways. You'll pick up a new guitar lick here, notice a new way to beat out rhythm on a percussion instrument there, learn the words to a song you didn't know from one individual, maybe even originate a new melody or tune of your own with someone else.

Don't let all this information get away from you! Start a notebook of song chords and fingerings and words and other musical knowledge and keep it by your side during each jam session you attend. That way it'll come in handy when you want to add something, or someone else wants to copy information from your book for his or her own use, or a real beginner just needs help with the words to a tune at a sing-along.

Old Time Fiddlers' jam session.

I find that I've enlarged my repertoire of songs a great deal faster since I've started taking my notebook to music parties. Without the book, I'm liable to forget a new tune almost as soon as I hear it. But if I immediately write the song's words down just once, I can often remember them afterwards without ever referrin gto the copy again.

Hank Bradley, Sue Thompson, and an unidentified fiddler. The instrument Hank is playing is a bazouki.

And that's important because new songs—not necessarily *new* new, just new to you—are the lifeblood of music. The next time you find yourself losing interest in your music or noting a lack of progress in your abilities, get out to a hoot and add another batch of songs to your repertoire. It's like learning to fly each time you pick up a new tune. Or any kind of useful information, for that matter. Want to learn how to play a particular lick? If you see someone else do it at a party, don't be afraid to ask how it's done. Likewise if you need to know how to repair an instrument, and so on, *ask*. It's a real thrill to make leaps forward, and those leaps frequently come easy at a musical get-together.

It's exciting, too, to share what you know at such fests. The more you give, the more you get back, and jamming—no matter what form it takes—is the most effective way I know for both teaching and learning what music's all about.

Music's first name is "people" ("It's all folk music—I ain't heard no hosses singin' it." —Louis "Satchmo" Armstrong or Big Bill Broonzy?), and the more people you get together with to pick and sing—and the more often you do it—the more you'll learn and the faster you'll become the musician you want to be.

"But Where Are Those Other Folk Musicians?"

I get a lot of letters from folks, though, saying things like, "I'm the only one in my neighborhood who plays an instrument. How can I get in touch with others who play?" I've been in the same spot myself, and I've got a few ideas to share on how to deal with this kind of musical dry spell.

You can get together anytime!

One thing I do is head on down to a club that advertises "open mike." In a large metropolitan area there are usually several to choose from. You can find one somewhere almost any night of the week. If you live a little farther out, though, you may just have to initiate your own get-together. With the number of people who are into playing music these days, chances are good that you can find a place to hold your jam session.

There are various ways the open mike can work. Some clubs (taverns, bars, restaurants, or coffeehouses) will hire a solo performer or a group that has a P.A. system to open the show. The performers play a set or so to get everyone in the mood, then sit down and invite others up to play. This system usually works better if there's some sort of organization to it. For instance, those who want to play can talk to the emcee before the show or while others are playing. A sign-up list with designated times can sometimes be helpful, depending on the number of people who want to play. The amount of time each performer gets may have to be limited so that everyone will get a chance. Any less than three songs or 15 minutes is too little, though. A picker needs to have a little time to get warmed up. Twenty minutes to a half an hour is better.

Another way I've seen it work is on the open-jam principle. Here the band will play a set and then invite people up to join in one or more tunes. Many times you'll find a combination of the two systems at work. Whichever way it's organized, an open-mike program seems to benefit everyone involved. The club's management has an opportunity to audition new talent; the band usually is guaranteed a large, enthusiastic audience (even on traditionally slack week nights); and local pickers have a chance to try out their new licks, while meeting fellow musicians and making new friends.

But you don't really need a P.A. system to get an open mike together. All you really need is a place, which could be your own living room, a local church, or a library. If you start in a small room, you won't need sound reinforcement. What I'm suggesting here is the formation of a song circle or folklore society. You can meet once a week, twice a month, or whenever you like. The important thing is to get together with others who want to share their music.

Plan weekly or monthly meetings and put up notices on the bulletin board at the post office, general store, or laundromat—wherever public notices are posted. In addition, you might like to submit a small written announcement of your plans to the local newspaper editor, who will probably be glad to print the item (as long as the event it describes is a nonprofit venture). Be sure, when doing this, to include the date and location of the jamboree, and a phone number that people can call for information.

Any organization or regular event needs a person or persons who put energy into it and keep it going. You may just be that person, if your love for music and need for new songs and musical influences is strong enough.

If you do happen to own a P.A. system, and don't mind the smoky bar atmosphere, you might consider approaching a local club owner with the idea of sponsoring an open mike. Besides starting a music scene, you may be able to help make your equipment pay for itself. You should certainly get paid for setting up the sound system and organizing the event, just as though you were the full-time entertainment. It would be a good idea, too, to make your own posters to put up around town to help see to it the word gets out. The club owner should be willing to share the printing cost, and might also want to place an advertisement announcing the event in the local newspaper.

Some clubs will want to do open mikes for their regular Friday or Saturday night entertainment. Others may want it on Sunday afternoon, Sunday evening, or a week night when business is slack. In some cases a club will want to purchase its own sound system for use on open-mike night. In this case the manager may need advice on what equipment is good, and will usually need to hire an emcee to run the show. (That could be you!)

One other thought on the subject: If your open mike is going to take place in a public place, I think it's a good idea to pick one that offers more than just beer and wine at the bar. A lot of us musicians just aren't into booze (we find we can get loose on the excitement of the jam alone!), and we would be happier with good ole fruit juice or tea. For that reason, a place such as a coffeehouse, which serves both alcohol and other beverages, may attract a wider range of customers.

Pass the Word

You've probably noticed by now that a major theme of this book is "making music a more important part of local culture." Another kind of musical promotion I've tried is conducting homegrown music workshops in which school children, scout troops, seniors, and folk festival fans of all ages can learn how easy it is to play a homemade music - maker. I take along a variety of instruments (such as washtub basses, jugs, spoons, washboards, musical saws, and kazoos) and demonstrate each one before passing it around for everyone to try. Then I provide musical accompaniment on guitar or banjo for the participants' first musical attempts.

I have also been known to *combine* the open-mike principle with the idea of the homemade music workshop. I bring the instrumetns and grab untrained (or otherwise inexperienced) volunteers from the audience to form a jug band. This can be quite a lot of fun, and many times I've "discovered" some talented person who never knew she or he could play the musical saw, tub bass, or whatever!

So there you have it, folks— a few ideas on how to get some local players together, have a good time, and "culturize" your community to boot! All it really takes is a little energy and enthusiasm to pass the word that music can be a lot of fun for *everybody*!

Making Money with Homegrown Music

SINCE almost anybody can use a few extra bucks every now and then, I'm going to plunge right in here and tell you how you might be able to turn your music hobby into an occasional job—to finance a new set of strings, pay for the gas on your trip to town, or even cover the rent check once in a while.

However, before you attempt to parlay your pickin' into cold hard cash, it's best to be sure that you've reached the point in your study of music where you feel like sharing it with folks other than close friends and relatives. (Trying to play professionally *before* your ability is up to the task can be a mighty disheartening experience!) And once you have enough proficiency at your chosen instrument to perform in public, you still need to find an audience that's willing to pay to be entertained.

I've been earning a share of my income by pickin' and singin' for several years, so I can make some suggestions that might just help you find a few of those paying listeners.

I'd like to point out right from the start, though, that I'm *not* promoting the notion that you can become self-sufficient by playing music. In most cases (the exceptions being mainly tiresome gigs in nightclubs or bars that will support you for a few months or so), the only way to actually earn a living from music is to spend a lot of time on the road.

Now, this sort of work could provide an acceptable life style for nomadic people who don't mind living in a truck or a school bus, but the constant wandering that it requires would be pretty much out of the question for homebodies who prefer to spend time around the homestead or farmstead. On the other hand, if you already keep your expenses to a minimum—perhaps by growing your own food or owning your own home—an occasional extra source of income may be all that you need. Either way, whether you hope to become a full-time pro or just aim to feed the cookie jar every once in a while, you'll probably have to start at the bottom.

Street-Singing

And that starting point, in terms of playing for pay, is the kind of gig that you don't

Street musician Harmonica Bruce and friends ply their trade. Bruce is playing through a portable amplifier hung around his neck.

have to audition for, because you hire yourself. I'm talking, of course, about singing on the street! There's usually not a whole lot of money in this sort of work. In fact $20 a day for three or four very strenuous sets is about the best you should expect, unless your act is extremely unusual and you happen to be playing during the Christmas season.

Remember, too, that for some strange reason it's illegal in many areas to just set yourself up on a corner and play. So unless you've seen other street acts on your intended spot, it's best to check with the police department before you start to perform. Many places (Seattle's Pike Place Market and the city of San Francisco, for example) require you to obtain a street-singer's license.

What you'll be doing, should you decide to try one of these do-it-yourself jobs, is singing and playing your heart out—with your hat, guitar case, or whatever opened invitingly—in hopes that people will brighten up and salt that container with a little spare change (or even an apple or an orange).

And don't feel that your unsolicited performance constitutes begging. The world can always use another song, and music on the streets adds a little culture to the urban environment.

The Small Restaurant Scene

For a variation on the above theme, you could try to sign up with a small restaurant, sandwich shop, or salad kitchen in exchange for a salary or even just tips and lunch. If you see a likely place that doesn't have a resident minstrel, approach the manager with your idea. It would probably be best to begin by offering your services in exchange for lunch and a small fee. Then, if the manager won't agree to that plan, he or she may at least be willing to guarantee a certain figure ($10 to $20 is probably as much as you can expect) and promise to make up the difference if your tips don't equal that amount.

Craft Carnivals and County Fairs

Better yet, if you get real tight with a bunch of your homegrown musical friends (and I don't mean after passing the bottle of home-brew around a few times), you might consider looking for work at a local craft carnival or similar affair. My group has just finished an extended tour of these festivals, and we closed off the season with our annual performance at the Western Washington State Fair.

In order to tackle this type of job, you should have a good, solid repertoire of at least 20 or 30 songs. The average set, you see, will consist of between 10 and 15 numbers (unless you get into long jams with extended solo breaks). Most craft carnivals or county fairs are good for one or two sets.

Watch out, though, for the old "We don't have much money left in our budget, but the exposure will do you good" routine. If your only goal is to get up and entertain people, this is one pleasant way among many to do it. And if you are just getting started, it *is* a way to let a lot of folks know about what you're doing. But that kind of arrangement can be overdone. If it goes on too long, you will begin to realize that you're providing a valuable service to the fair's management and receiving nothing (or next to it) in return.

Promoting Your Own Concert

You (or your band) could promote your *own* concert or dance. This idea should work especially well in a rural area, where there often isn't much entertainment available and where buildings such as grange halls can usually be rented at reasonable rates. If you start from scratch in this way, however, you'll have to advertise. The best and least expensive way to do this is to find a graphic artist (there may even be one in your group) to make some simple posters that you can have photocopied. You need to get these promotional materials out where folks can see them at least two weeks before the event, and you need to make sure that the local newspapers and radio stations know about your hoedown, too. Such sources will often give you free publicity *if* you get the materials to them well in advance of the performance.

Your self-promoted shindig will be a whole lot more likely to succeed if you can avoid competing with other public entertainments, such as the big movies, local high school dances, and so on. Foreknowledge of other big events isn't always available, however, so you'll have to be ready to just break even — or maybe go into the hole — unless you're able to assure attendance at your concert or dance by selling advance tickets.

Sometimes the local movie theater may be useful to you. Theater owners are occasionally willing to run a live music show—perhaps at no cost to the musicians—

Try a gig at your local craft fair or county fair.

because of the money they can make selling refreshments during the performance. Since the theater owner ordinarily has to *pay* to show a film (and may be having trouble with attendance on week nights), this sort of symbiotic arrangement with a live band could be to the owner's advantage.

Weddings and Parties

Weddings and private parties also offer income possibilities to the homegrown musician. All of the job-finding methods mentioned above will help you get invited to play at such occasions, and you might also have some business cards printed. These "pocket posters" shouldn't cost too much money, and can be hung in all the places where you see other cards (the ones that advertise bulldozing, horseshoeing, remodeling, and so forth) tacked up, or just handed out to anyone who expresses an interest in hiring you or your group.

Booking a Community College Concert

If you feel that your solo act or group really has something special to offer, why not try to book a concert at a small college? Many of the junior colleges that have sprung up everywhere over the last few years offer their students free entertainment programs during the day (often during lunch hours), or evening concerts. In order to get one of these jobs, though, you may have to put together what's known as a *promo package*. This packet will usually contain a photograph of you or your group, a record or tape recording of a few of your tunes, and a glowing description of the kind of performance you put on. A poster—

which the college could make copies of to place around the campus—would also be a big help.

Junior college jobs weren't hard to come by a few years back. Now, however (at least around my area), you have to have your promo kit in the mailbox by the end of the school year in order to get booked for either of the following two semesters. The community colleges in your locale may not be so sophisticated yet. Call the colleges you're interested in and ask to talk to the student entertainment coordinator. Tell that person about your group and inquire about the booking policy.

The Promo Package

A promo package serves two purposes—to advertise your act to prospective bookers and to advertise your performance, once booked, to the public. My original promo package contained a photocopied poster with a couple of pictures and the slogan "Homegrown Mountain Music," and a short typed description of the kind of music I play. After a while I had a newspaper clipping to add from an article that ran in the local daily paper about my escapades in a nearby sandwich shop. Even with this crude kit, I was able to get $50 for a one-hour performance—and many folks with better packages were getting a good deal more.

What might better packages consist of, you ask? Well, first, a good 8-by-10 black-and-white glossy photograph with plenty of pizazz. This probably won't be an action shot, partly because good action shots are hard to get. (If you've got one, use it.) One reason for having a good photograph is that it helps you get space in a local paper. Editors will use a good photograph sometimes even if they couldn't care less about the news value of your upcoming performance, simply because it helps make their page look more interesting. Why, my group ended up right there next to an ad for the movie *Jaws* one time, even though we were relatively unknown in Seattle then, just because our photograph was a masterpiece (done by a friend who had worked in New York for such respected establishments as *Vogue* magazine). There are various features that make a good promo picture, and I recommend using an experienced photographer—one who has worked print media (perhaps a local newspaper), if you can find and afford one.

A press release announcing your upcoming performance is another important item for your package. Think what you'd like to read about yourself in an article in the local paper. Now write the article yourself and type it, double-spaced, on 8½-by-11 white paper, and title it "For Immediate Release." If your band has letterhead or a logo, use it. Run off some copies on as good a copier as you can find—you want the piece to look professional. If the article is good, many times the editor will spruce it up a bit and run it as though he'd written it himself.

Of course, a press release is no substitute for an article written by a reporter who's actually heard you, so you should do everything you can to get that, too. The press release is only the first step. Keeping the right reporter posted on your whereabouts is step two. Put him or her on your mailing list.

Mailing list? Well, you need one of these when you really start getting serious—when you start getting booked for two or three months ahead. Every place you play, put out a legal pad and encourage your diehard fans to write their names, addresses, and phone numbers on it. Then publish a newsletter every three months that includes your schedule for the next three, to send around to your fans and all the media people who could help you. But even if you've only got one gig, write a release and send it out to all the media people.

An example of a successful promo picture. This photo of the Okie Doke Band has appeared in several newspapers. (Author is seated at right.)

The third important item in the promo kit is a record or a tape that will serve as an audition for some prospective bookers, such as colleges. Others will ask for a live audition or will come out to see you. Once you develop a following, a record or a cassette tape you can sell will sometimes serve a dual purpose: money from sales might pay the expenses of producing the recording (and you might even make a profit!), and a record or tape for sale is much more impressive as an audition than one made only for promotion.

The really slick acts that perform in the college-concert circuit package their promo kits in personalized folders, sometimes using a folder printed especially for one performance or run. That kind of packaging can be really expensive, though, and with a little inventiveness and judicious use of copy machines, you can turn out attractive and serviceable publicity materials at a much lower cost.

Should You Electrify Yourself?

If you have an acoustic solo act or group, it's unlikely that you'll need your own sound-amplifying equipment for most of the jobs that I've mentioned. If you need this paraphernalia, it will be provided by the sponsoring organization. Of course, a sound system would definitely expand your performing possibilities, but unless you're a good and patient "horse trader" or know how to build the equipment yourself, a sound system can be very expensive. If you live near a music store, you may be able to rent the equipment when you need your own sound reinforcement. Playing and singing through a microphone, by the way, is a whole different procedure from playing and singing without one. The microphone is essentially an instrument, too, and it takes some practice to make it sound right, just as it does to many any other instrument sound good. Whenever possible you should also take along someone to "do sound" for you when you're playing an amplified gig—someone who can balance everything, make tonal adjustments, and tell you if you're projecting through the microphone properly. Obviously, the person for this job should be someone who knows your music and understands how it's supposed to sound.

Since sound-reinforcement equipment is expensive, you'll probably have to find a way to finance it. If the group plans to stay together, one way would be to earmark a percentage of the fee for each gig to make payments on the equipment. Another plan would be for each member of the group to buy a particular piece of equipment, and another would be for each member to invest an equal amount of money to buy the system outright, and to be paid back from a certain percentage of each gig.

Bars and Taverns

If you have your own sound system, bars and taverns are perhaps the most obvious opportunity of all. The problem with these gigs is that you usually have to play twice as long as at a concert, usually in a smoke-filled room, for less money than you would make at a concert. On the positive side, these places can offer steady work—or if not "steady," several nights as opposed to once-a-year shots at fairs. If you have a large following (if you are a good dance band, for instance), these gigs can be a lot of fun. I guess the ultimate question is, would you be there anyway, dancing and having a good time? If so, why not get paid for doing it? If not, it may be hard to get into the spirit and enjoy that kind of work.

If you want to spread the good feelings that you get from music around—performing by yourself or with your pickin' partners—check out a few of the scenes that I've described. The opportunities are there, and more can be created! Just believe that the world should have more music, and you'll begin to see the places where that need exists.

7

Doing Your Own Recording at Home

EVER wish that little cassette recorder in your cabin was a $1,000 stereo system? I know a couple of tricks to make it sound a whole lot more like one.

Generally the circuitry in portable cassette recorders is capable of much more accurate sound reproduction than the small built-in speakers and microphones they come with will deliver. It's really surprising what happens when you connect a high-fidelity speaker system to the earphone jack, for instance.

What's a high-fidelity speaker system? Well, this kind of system used to be stock equipment in big cabinet-model black and white TVs—the ones with the big grill cloth across the bottom. Most of the picture tubes are dead now, but the cabinets are so nice, it's hard to throw them in the dump, so many are sitting out in a garage, basement, or similar junk room, unless the owners have broken down finally and hauled them to the dump. You can often find two or three at a dump, as well as old hi-fi speakers for record players. I've also found old bookshelf-style stereo speakers at the dump. Even car radio speakers would make some improvement in the sound of your portable recorder.

You don't have to remove the speaker from the (TV) cabinet unless the cabinet is too big for your space. If it is, you can build a smaller box for the speaker, which is usually mounted with four screws or bolts. You can cut the wires if necessary or, if they end in a plug, you can get an adapter to convert to the plug you'll need, or leave them long if you can use them to connect the speaker to your radio. If you do remove the speaker, you should consider recycling the cabinet. I made a fruit dryer out of one. I've also seen these cabinets holding children's toys.

You need a special cord to test the speakers. To make one, all you need is a length of speaker-connecting wire four to six feet long, a couple of alligator clips, and a miniature phone jack. You can get these inexpensive items at almost any electronics supply house or stereo shop. Your total investment should be around $3.

You can either solder the connectors to the appropriate ends of the wire or buy solderless connectors, with screws to wrap the wires around. Alternatively, you could attach a mini-plug to the end of the wires already soldered to the speaker you want to test, or solder your wires to the speaker terminals rather than using alligator clips. If you use alligator clips, you can test several speakers with one cord.

My own speaker-recycling experience began when a neighbor gave me an old, discarded TV. I removed the guts, taking great care with the picture tube. (Picture tubes are like bombs—I set this one very gently in the bottom of a 55-gallon drum, then threw a big rock into the drum from as far away as I could.) If you're so inclined, you can salvage electronic parts and hardware, as well as speakers, from these kinds of old appliances.

Then I hooked the earphone jack of my portable cassette recorder/radio to the terminals of the 10-inch hi-fi speaker in the cabinet and was amazed by the power and range of the sounds that came forth. These larger speakers are so much more efficient than the little ones in the portables (partly because they have larger magnets) that they give an enormous increase in volume. Not only does the little machine have the power to drive the speakers, but it sounds like a much more efficient unit.

Patching

You can patch portable radios and cassette recorders into your stereo and get better sound from the little machine. If you want to do this, connect the earphone or external speaker jack to the AUX input of the amplifier using a *shielded* cable to reduce AC hum. You can buy manufactured cords with a mini-plug on one end and the phono plug on the other, since you don't want the cord to be attached to your speakers permanently.

You can improve the recording quality of a small recorder, too, by connecting a better microphone to the external mike input. Most good microphones don't have a miniature jack on their cords, but you can get an adapter or use a microphone mixer. A mixer allows you to get a certain amount of recording studio quality when you record a group of musicians. Try it out.

Recording Homegrown Tunes

Many times in your music-making career you have probably felt that your performance of a certain tune or collection of songs was worth preserving. (If you're just getting started, I'm sure there *will* be such times.) Since it's often hard to tune in on your partners while you're concentrating on your own instrument, perhaps you just wanted to hear what the total sound of your group was like. Maybe you needed an audition tape to send to producers and club managers, or perhaps you wanted to have a record or tape to sell at your gigs.

Whatever the reason for the urge to record, you'll be glad to know that it's easier to preserve your music than many folks think. You can even do it yourself in your own home!

Although most people believe that superior recordings can be produced only in a professional studio that's equipped with the latest high-priced gizmos, the fact is that excellent recordings can be made under much simpler conditions. (Some of the best tracks I've heard were taped in homes by musicians using borrowed equipment.)

A living room recording session.

Technology has advanced so quickly in the past few years that a person can now make a better-quality recording on his or her home stereo deck than was possible on even the best commercial equipment available 20 years ago.

It's true that musicians may be able to hear themselves better in a studio, and may be inspired, as a result, to turn out a more enthusiastic performance—but the same professional setting can easily bring about a tense recording session. Since they are paying an hourly studio rental fee—which can range from a reasonable $15 to as high as $100—performers in such a situation are likely to feel rushed, and may find it difficult to produce their best music.

Since in-home recording can be done out from under that kind of time pressure, instead of spending money to rent a studio for a few hours, you might get a better product by borrowing or renting a few pieces of equipment and record at home. Even if you plan to do your final recording in a studio, it's always a good idea to practice your arrangements in front of the microphones at home *before* you start that expensive tape rolling. Who knows: You may be so pleased with the results of your rehearsal tapes that you will decide to skip the studio altogether!

You could even make the master tape at home (or at a live performance), where you can take your time and get it just right, then take your tape to a commercial studio for professional mixing and equalizing. Or you could record the basic tracks in an inexpensive studio, then take the tape to a better-equipped one for final mixing and mastering.

Of course, there's a limit to how much noise can be eliminated and bad tone balance corrected, but often home sessions will produce a more inspired performance. From my point of view, the performance is the most important part of the recording, with technical perfection being secondary. In my opinion, the ultraperfection of many modern recordings is actually detrimental to the feeling in the music. You'll see what I mean if you'll listen to a remake of a classic song from the 50s or 60s, then listen to the original.

Taping Tips

EQUIPMENT

So how do you give homemade recordings a sharp and clear professional quality? Well, simply by using top-notch equipment and the proper mixing techniques. Obviously, you'll want to get hold of the very best tape recorder and microphones you can lay your hands on, but you'll also need a good mike mixer (if you plan to record more than one instrument at a time) and a good playback system.

The mixer—which is used for adjusting relative sound levels of different instruments and voices—could be one of those normally used for stage mixing, as long as it has a "mic" level output. Ideally, your playback system should be able to reproduce accurately the whole audio range, so that your recording will sound good on everything from an expensive stereo system to a blaring car radio. It's important not to listen to your playback only on headphones because the music may sound quite different when it comes from speakers, and the way it sounds through speakers determines the way the recording should be mixed.

I've found that, although there is a good deal of difference between expensive recording microphones and moderately priced stage mikes, you can get very good results in a home recording session with these stage mikes. My friend Phil Williams (who is co-owner of his own record company, Voyager Recordings) says, however, that you can actually get better sound quality from condenser mikes than from dynamic mikes in the same price range.

Your best bet, when choosing recording equipment, is to obtain a reel-to-reel setup, because it's easy to duplicate reel tapes and the recordings made on them are generally of a higher quality than those made on cassettes, since the reel machines record at faster tape speeds than cassette recorders do. A multitrack unit will offer more versatility and is particularly desirable if you plan to have your tape mixed professionally later.

The faster the tape moves, the better its sound reproduction will be, so use a machine that moves at a speed of at least 7½ inches per second. (Many commercial studios now use systems that can record at 30 ips!) The better the quality of the tape, the less "fuzz" (surface noise) you will get, so buy the best tape you can afford. Some machines require adjustments for different brands of tape, so be sure to consult the operator's guide for your recording system.

ENVIRONMENT

A way to cut background noise, if you're not in a professional studio, is to make sure that motors such as refrigerators and heater fans are turned off while you are rolling tape. These devices can create both audible noise and electrical disturbances that will be "heard" by the recording circuits of your tape machine. If the wiring in your house is old, or inadequately grounded, you may have to look for another place to stage your session to avoid this kind of noise.

If you don't have a mixer or are short on mikes, and are recording two or more instruments, with some players sharing a microphone, you can either experiment with placing the musicians at different distances from the mikes, or have the performers vary their volume. Another possibility is to have players step up to the mike for solos and step back for backup playing, a technique from the old days of radio and recording. Obviously, one of the luxuries of home recording is that it allows you time to experiment in order to find just the right mix (whereas, in a studio, you're dependent on the engineer's knowledge to avoid spending time on such variables).

The room you record your music in can have as much effect on the quality of your sound as the microphones you use. Different sized rooms make recordings sound different, and varying amounts of sound-absorbing material, such as carpets and furniture, will affect the resonance of a room. You might experiment with just one microphone and one voice or instrument in different rooms, recording them, then listening to the results. The sound you get can also be affected by how far the mike is from the source of sound, partly because the farther away it is, the more room sound you get.

RECORDING ENGINEER

This is the sort of thing recording engineers go to school to learn, and where their experience pays off. When you are recording at home, it's best to have as knowledgeable a person as possible around to listen and fiddle with knobs while you are concentrating on your playing. This person doesn't have to be a trained engineer, though you can often hire one for much less than studio recording time, which generally includes the engineer's services. Perhaps you have a friend with a discerning ear, or know a fellow musician who has a good idea what the music should sound like and what good tone is.

The room and the sound system both affect your playback quality, so it's a good idea to listen to your recording on several systems, to help you find out what the idiosyncrasies of your setup are so that you can make adjustments to get better sound.

A Home-Recording Co-op

Another idea that may help you make better home recordings is to start a co-op! Get several people together who want to record their songs and are willing to pool equipment. One person may own a good four-track (or better) tape deck; another may have a good microphone; a third may agree to buy a mixing board; and a fourth may agree to acquire an echo unit—whatever your imagination can work out. One member may have a basement that the group can convert into a studio, perhaps by installing egg cartons or other sound-absorbent material on walls and ceiling and carpeting the floor. Everybody could help out on everybody else's recordings, playing backup instruments, singing, engineering, or whatever. Not only would it be fun, but you could turn out much

This is how your basement recording studio might look. Egg cartons on the wall provide acoustic insulation.

higher quality tapes at lower cost to each participant than you could on your own, if you had to own all the equipment. It's a great way to get some experience playing producer, too!

The Cassette Mass Market

Once you've successfully mastered the fundamentals of recording your tunes on a home sound stage, you may want to go into mass production of your recordings. If so, you should consider duplicating your original tape on cassettes. Even though cassettes are not ideal for doing the original recording, they are a fine way to release your music to the public at a reasonably low cost to you.

Since many people own cassette players and the sound reproduction of these players is good, cassette recordings successfully compete with phonograph records in today's music market. The primary marketing disadvantage of cassettes, of course, is the lack of space on the package for cover photographs and liner notes, features that help sell an album, but lack of space means that your printing costs will be lower than they would be for an album.

Record-it-yourselfers can find a source of real inspiration and guidance in *How to Make and Sell Your Own Record*, by Diane Sward Rapaport, the first definitive work on the subject. (See the book listings in the *Resources* section for the address of the publisher.) Although it's certainly not a technical manual on record engineering (a couple of those *are* available from Musician's Supply, in the *Resources* section on mail-order suppliers), the book does describe the various pieces of recording equipment and their uses.

The book's strong point is its overview of the *whole* process of making a record, including promotion and marketing. Moving backwards, the text takes up the promotion and sales of a finished album first, then discusses the printing and manufacturing phases before it gets to the original planning and recording of a disc. The reason for this order is that you *should* think first about how you're going to market your record if selling copies is a primary object of producing it. For instance, marketing may influence which tunes you do and the order in which you arrange them on the record.

Some folks produce records or cassette tapes primarily to use for promotion. But considering the expense of making an original recording, it's certainly worth your while to think about making it marketable and producing enough copies for sale to recover at least some of your investment. From your first recording experience, you will certainly learn things that will help you make a better one the second time. This is what Rapaport thinks, and if you use the work sheets that accompany each chapter in her book, you will be totally organized as soon as you've worked your way through the process once.

A Success Story

To inspire you, I'd like to tell you about a couple who have been recording their own music—mostly old-time fiddling—for over 15 years! Phil and Vivian Williams started Voyager Recordings by taping in the field (literally!) with very simple gear at "parking-lot" jam sessions during the National Old Time Fiddling Championships held around the third week in June each year in Weiser, Idaho. They've gradually updated their "studio" until they now have about $5,000 worth of equipment, nearly all of which was purchased secondhand from radio stations and pawnshops, and through newspaper ads.

Phil and Vivian record "live" performances at festivals or right in their own living room, and their large catalog testifies to the variety of good-quality music that can be put out on a shoestring. The Voyager lineup includes lots of Vivian's award-winning fiddlin', plus the old-time string-band sounds of The Old Hat Band, the Texas-style fiddle-playing of Benny Thomassen, and the plain ole foot-stompin' music of Rag Daddy. Lots of other styles are evident, too, from bluegrass to African marimba music. (See the record company section of *Resources* for Voyager's address.)

Phil used to engineer all his own releases, but recently he hired an experienced engineer to twiddle knobs and set up microphones, with what he says are astounding results. He uses the same equipment as before, but apparently the engineer's experience counts! Phil says paying the engineer doesn't really strain the budget, either, which (as of 1980) allowed $2,500 per album, including pressing the records and printing the covers.

Contrary to what you might think, the Williamses haven't made a lot of money from producing and selling their own records. What little profit they do make is automatically rechanneled to finance future releases. As Phil explains, "We don't do it to make money. We do it because we want to, because we feel this music *should* be recorded and made available to those who like it."

Writing Your Own Tunes

HAVE you ever wished someone would write a song that expresses your personal feelings, beliefs, and interests? Well then, grab your guitar, or take a seat at the piano, and work up a song of your own! The fact is that you can compose a tune even if you've never tried it. Song-writing isn't really as difficult as it may seem. After all, anything that's part of *your* life—how you feel, what you see, or someone you care for—is worth singing about! as it may seem. After all, anything that's part of *your* life—how you feel, what you see, or someone you care for—is worth singing about!

All you need to start writing songs (besides the urge to express a particular feeling) is some notion of how a song is structured. If you already play other people's tunes, you probably know how music is put together, and even if you are a novice musician, you can learn song structure by simply learning a few songs all the way through.

Musical ABC's

As an aid to aspiring tunesmiths, I've prepared descriptions of some of the building blocks of a song. Once you're familiar with the fundamentals, you can experiment with them in countless ways to create your own one-of-a-kind piece of music.

Lyrics—the words of a song—are usually divided into versus, a chorus (refrain), and sometimes a bridge, which provides a transition between verse/chorus sections. If you have a specific thought to express, you'll probably need to write lyrics, but music can also communicate emotions quite effectively with its melody alone.

Chord progression is the underlying harmonic structure of the piece of music. It is a series of chords that supports the melody and supplies *harmony*.

Two other elements of music are *rhythm* and *tempo*. Rhythm is the alternating pattern of strong and weak accents in a melodic line. Although you can have rhythm without melody, even in pieces of African music that are all percussion, there are melodic things happening. Harmony, in fact, is actually rhythmic, since two notes are harmonious because they have similar rhythmic vibrations. Tempo is simply the rate of speed at which a song is performed as measured by a metronome in beats per minute.

Once you can comfortably work with the fundamentals of music, you might wonder how to put them all together to make a song. Is it best, for instance, to write the lyrics first and then devise a melody around them, or vice versa? Or should you wait for it all to come to you at once, in a blinding flash of genius?

Well, there's no rule that applies to all cases since every musician has his or her own way of writing songs. I've written most of mine by thinking of the words first and then setting them to music, but in some of my best creations the words and music came out all at once, while I was sitting around strumming my guitar and making up phrases as I went along. I know a number of folks who write all the music first, and then fit words to it. It's common for songwriters to collaborate — one writing the lyrics while the other writes the music. Sometimes one partner will make up one line and the other will write the next.

The Key to It All

Although there are plenty of different chord progressions, rhythms, and fancy time signatures that you could experiment with, I'd advise you, if you are a novice songwriter, not to worry about all that in the beginning. Your first important task is to find a key you can sing in comfortably while accompanying yourself on your favorite instrument. As you experiment, you'll likely find several keys that will be your favorites, so that the one you choose will depend on how it suits the particular melody. You'll also need to choose a key that mirrors the message of your lyrics. A minor key normally conveys quiet, sad emotions, while a major key generally makes a song sound happy and boisterous.

Contrary to what a lot of people think, the key is not usually named for the note the song starts on, but rather for the note that it resolves into, or ends on. Many songs modulate, or change key, in midflight, but such tricks are not essential. They function primarily as ear-catchers. Any key will offer you a wide selection of chords on which to build the melody, so it pays to know — from listening carefully to songs you're familiar with — which chords belong to which keys, and just how they work together.

Now that bit of self-education doesn't have to be as complicated as it sounds. In fact, many good American folk songs use no more than two chords! A good example is the well-known "Polly Wolly Doodle": In the key of C all you need are the C chord and the G chord. If you'd rather do it in G, the chords are G and D. This classic song also offers a demonstration of how many talented musicians (Woody Guthrie, for example) put their lyrics together. It's easy to make up new verses for a simple melody by tacking on rhymed couplets with the appropriate number of syllables and accents in each line. Try it yourself!

The Proper Mind Set

Beyond mastering and practicing the musical fundamentals of writing songs, a tunesmith needs to develop a frame of mind that is always receptive to the makings of a

Marc Bristol performing original tunes at a cafe.

worthwhile song. Train your mind to regard *everything* around you as potential material. Simply returning from a long trip once prompted me to compose a song to express the strong emotion I always feel about coming home. Most people who really enjoy song-writing, I've noticed, have this "always-on-the-lookout" attitude.

To turn experience and events into good songs, you have to learn to be observant. As you develop the ability to "see" things musically, you might want to exercise your ability by making up verses to existing songs. Then, when you think you've got a really good idea for an original piece, don't be afraid to *work* on it. Just plunge ahead and start trying out verses and melodies. The tune might come easily, and it might not. Either way, you'll be thrilled when you finally have the whole song ready to pull out of the bag and sing when you feel like communicating the feeling it expresses or the story it tells.

As you work, bear in mind the *goal* of your song. Do you want to dance to it, or sing the children to sleep? Do you need to heal a pain in your heart? Do you wish to create or celebrate a heroic deed? Do you want to express your love for someone, or your fear of something? Focus on the purpose, and that will help your song to flow more easily. If you know what you want to say through your music, the details will come on the strength of your desire to communicate and your perseverance at the task.

Make It Legal

Even though your compositions might be intended only for your own entertainment, or that of your family and friends, there may come a time, as you gain confidence in your song-writing, when you'll decide to record an original tune or two. If so, you'll need legal protection for the piece—after all, you wouldn't want another musician to pick up your work and make a fortune from it while giving you no credit at all! Judging from my mail, it seems that a lot of folks are worried about theft, so let me review the different ways a songwriter can publish and protect original compositions.

In theory, you own the legal rights to any song you compose as soon as it's committed to paper or preserved on tape or record. But you also need to register the song to prove when you composed it. The most obvious way to do this—and the method you should use if you're sure your tune will be released to the public on a tape or record—is to register it with the Library of Congress Office of Copyrights.

To do so, just fill out the correct form (which you can obtain free from the Register of Copyrights, Library of Congress, Washington, D.C. 20559), pay a $10 fee, and submit either a lead sheet (containing the melody, chords, and lyrics) *or* a recorded version of the composition. Make sure any recordings you submit are very clear, and—if you're releasing the piece yourself—send two copies to the Office of Copyrights.

Should you have several tunes to register, you might want to avoid paying a separate registration fee for each one by publishing a collection of songs in a single volume and registering them all under the title of the book. (A variation on this is to string all the numbers together as a suite.) Such procedures are perfectly all right, but I recommend that each piece be registered under its own title if it's going to become a recorded release. Proper copyright notice must be affixed to printed copies. The form is

©1982 Marc Bristol. All rights reserved.

For published music, use copyright symbol ©. On sound recordings, use ℗.

The Value of Song-Writing

You may be wondering why you should take the trouble to set your innermost thoughts and feelings to music and then offer them up for public consumption. Well, it's impossible to predict the effect that your songs could have on other folks. The Beatles demonstrated the profound effect that a songwriter—or a group of musicians—can have on society. When John Lennon died, even Radio Moscow played a 90-minute concert of his peace-promoting music. And Arlo Guthrie's "Alice's Restaurant Massacre" may have been the single most effective antiwar protest song written in recent years. It's a sure bet that there are plenty of important causes nowadays that could use all our musical energies. In fact, many present-day folk singers are turning their attention—and their creativity—to the antinuclear movement.

However, the most important reason for writing music, in my opinion, is that it tends

to bond us all to one another and to the earth that sustains us. Songs, because they become part of history, are the lifeblood of cultural tradition. And they come directly from folks, like you and me, who are trying to share feelings and insights with their neighbors. Since life styles are changing almost daily, the older songs of our culture sometimes can't mirror the particular outlook of the present generation.

And finally, besides providing the opportunity to make an important social statement, homegrown tunes—with their emotional content—are just plain good medicine for the soul!

Attending Folk Music Festivals

SEVERAL years back I was really taken by the theme music for a new television series called *The Beverly Hillbillies*. The "new" sound that was catching my ear was the banjo of Earl Scruggs. Earl caught a lot of folks' ears, and by the time he'd done the theme music for the movie *Bonnie and Clyde*, nearly everyone knew that bluegrass music is up-tempo country music featuring lots of sparkling banjo and fiddle work.

About that same time this country was enjoying a bit of a fok music revival with a lot of artists like the Kingston Trio, Pete Seeger, the New Lost City Ramblers, Joan Baez, and Bob Dylan getting national atteniton. During this era the folk festival idea was born, and the Newport Folk Festival was one of the first major annual events. Promoters of these events sometimes went to great lengths to rediscover talented folks who were living lives of obscurity out here in the real world. They didn't have to look far to find Bill Monroe, "the father of bluegrass," since Bill was still a popular feature of the Grand Ole Opry shows in Nashville, Tennessee.

Bluegrass Horizons

Bluegrass music got its name in the early 40s from Bill Monroe's backup bands, the Bluegrass Boys, but its origin goes farther back than that. Old-time string-band music was the popular form for dancing in the southern hills of Kentucky where Bill Monroe was born and raised, and Bill came from a family of musicians who traditionally played that music. Bill started off early backing his uncle Pen Vandiver on guitar for local dances. (Uncle Pen was later enshrined in one of Bill's most famous songs.)

Later, Bill and his brother Charlie landed a job doing vocal duets with Charlie on the guitar and Bill on mandolin. This early vocal sound of the Monroe Brothers is the soul of bluegrass music. Later, after Bill and Charlie drifted apart, Bill began experimenting with his backup sound. It wasn't until the later 40s, when he hired Lester Flatt and Earl Scruggs, that the banjo became so prominent in the genre.

Earl was using a three-finger technique on his banjo, which wasn't unheard of, especially in the North Carolina neighborhood he was from, but the driving, syncopated sound he got was new, and it set the music on fire. Lester and Earl eventually got tired of being on the road with Bill and broke off to form their own act, the Foggy Mountain Boys, but Bill's music had been unalterably changed. The banjo players in Bill's bands to this day play in Earl's style, and the name *Scruggs* is synonymous with bluegrass banjo.

Elizabeth Cotton, composer of the song "Freight Train, Freight Train" in concert at a folk festival.

More recently Earl teamed up with his sons playing banjo-flavored rock-and-roll under the name Earl Scruggs Revue. While the purists may be outraged, combining the two styles is perfectly all right with me. Besides the fact that it's really nice that they can all work together and bridge the generation gap like that, it was experimentation that gave birth to bluegrass in the first place, and to deny the right to experiment is contrary to the whole notion of American music. Our culture is a combination of a wide variety of elements, and the success of these experiments encourages cooperation around the world.

Several of the many graduates of Bill Monroe's Bluegrass Boys in the last 40 years have gone on to make names for themselves. If you like the sound of bluegrass music, many of these names are worth looking for either on records or at concerts. Jimmy Martin, for instance. Jimmy was lead vocalist and guitarist with Bill in the late 40s and early 50s and went on to form his own band, the Sunny Mountain Boys. Although he's been ostracized by purists for using drums in his band, Jimmy Martin has done some of the best bluegrass-style music I've heard. I'd have to call him a favorite.

Old Time Fiddlers stage at the Northwest Regional Folklife Festival.

Cross-breeding Audiences for Bluegrass and Country Music

I first heard Jimmy's voice and songs on an album called *Will the Circle Be Unbroken*, by the Nitty Gritty Dirt Band. The Dirt Band had been playing bluegrass and various other forms of country music for young people, and the manager got the idea that if he recorded his group on the same album with several of the stars of traditional country music, some important barriers might be broken down. The idea behind the album was to introduce two groups of people who were interested in two different styles of country music and thereby cross-breed the audiences.

With this in mind he rounded up Roy Acuff, Maybelle Carter, Doc Watson, Earl Scruggs, Pete "Brother Oswald" Kirby, Jimmy Martin, Merle Travis, Vassar Clements, and others in a studio in Nashville for a series of sessions with the Nitty Gritty Dirt Band. The result is a classic album—a three-record set cut all live and mixed on the spot. One whole side of this set is devoted to "breakdowns," or bluegrass instrumental tunes, and the others are full of wonderful renditions of classic songs by the above-mentioned luminaries, together with Jeff Hanna, Jimmie Fadden, Jim Ibbotson, John McEuen, and Les Thompson—the Dirt Band. If you were going to buy only one album of country music for your collection, this would be a good choice.

If you become an avid collector and aficionado of country music, here are a few more names to look for: "Uncle Josh" Graves is a fine dobro player, who has played and recorded with both Bill Monroe and Flatt and Scruggs, as well as doing albums on his own. If you are a big fan of dobro, as I am, you would also enjoy the playing of Mike Auldridge—much of which you may have heard in tracks by Emmylou Harris, Linda Ronstadt, and others. (Mike has solo albums on several labels.)

Jim and Jesse McReynolds are another brother vocal-harmony duet that can't be beat for that high lonesome sound. Vassar Clements, the fiddler, appeared on several of Jim and Jesse's country hits (yes, bluegrass occasionally has made the country charts). Vassar also played with Bill Monroe and went on to broaden the style of his music. Vassar is a powerful instrumentalist, and while his recent material is more in a rock and jazz vein, he hasn't lost my attention.

There are a good number of older groups to mention in bluegrass—the Stanley Brothers, the Osborne Brothers, Don Reno and the Tennessee Cutups, Mac Wiseman, Buck White, and many others. A new generation of bluegrass players have been making names for themselves as well, some favoring a traditional sound and others leaning to the experimental. Here are some names: Country Gazette, Hot Rize, Larry McNeely, Jack Skinner, Byron Berline, the New Cache Valley Drifters, the Newgrass Revival and Peter Rowen. There are a great many others.

Promoting Your Own Bluegrass Festival

The bluegrass festival has become an important phenomenon around the country, with more festivals popping up each year. They are great places to make contact with this music, and to hear some of the musicians mentioned above as well as local grassers—they're nearly everywhere by now. If there's not a regular bluegrass festival in your neck of the woods, you might think of starting one. All it takes is an appropriate location (with plenty of camping space if it's to last longer than one day) and someone with a lot of energy and organizational ability.

One thing I'd like to do is encourage the promoters of bluegrass events to try and keep an open mind. Variety is the spice of life, and without experimentation bluegrass would never have been born. Let's see some string swing bands, jug bands, solo performers, musical saws, and other forms of acoustic or nondeafening country music in addition to those traditional Bill Monroe-style sounds. You'll widen your audience for bluegrass if you widen the scope of your own taste a bit. Don't forget, by discouraging experimentation you may be (unsuccessfully I'll wager) attempting to quash the birth of some new form of music as wonderful as bluegrass, which would certainly have due respect for its ancestors.

Finding Folk Music Festivals

Starting with a bluegrass festival in Arizona in January, there are a wide variety of homegrown-music events throughout the year, all around the country. Many are scheduled when the weather is likely to be good so that they can be held outdoors, the better to accommodate large numbers of music lovers. Some festivals are devoted to fiddling or banjo-picking contests, and some are folk-dancing get-togethers. There are a few dulcimer gatherings, a guitar flat-picking championship, and other specialized events. Some are free to the public, and others have admission charges. Some are located near camping facilities. Frequently there are open-mike stages at these festivals where anyone can get up and do a few tunes.

One gathering I particularly like is the annual musical saw festival in Santa Cruz, California. Santa Cruz is especially exciting because amateur sawyers play right alongside such record-cutting professionals as Margaret Steinbuch, Moses Josiah, Robert Armstrong (who plays with the Cheap Suit Serenaders and recorded the theme for the movie *One Flew Over the Cuckoo's Nest*), and the festival's originator, Tom Scribner (who's played with the likes of Leon Russell and George Harrison, and been honored by having a bronze statue of himself, playing a saw, erected in Santa Cruz park).

The first day of the festival is filled with workshops and performances, followed by an evening show featuring the star performers. At the end of each year's gala evening show, all the saw players, amateur and pro, are gathered onstage for the finale. Here's what Tom Scribner wrote about that grand finale:

> When a massed bank of possibly a hundred or more saws cuts loose, God Almighty, the pigs will quit littering, coyotes will quit whelping, and the timber wolves will head for the tall uncut. . . . The noise may not be heavenly, but it certainly will be UNEARTHLY!!!

The second day of the festival features more informal performances, and mostly a get-together and picnic for everyone. The whole experience is thoroughly wonderful. It happens each year around Labor Day. For this year's schedule and other information, you can write to Festival of the Saws (see the folk music publications list in the *Resources* section for the address).

A broad-based folk festival that always features bluegrass in addition to a wide range of other traditional forms is the National Folk Festival, held each year at Wolf Trap Farm in Vienna, Virginia. The festival is put on by an organization called the National Council for the Traditional Arts. This organization also occasionally publishes a large directory of annual festivals (see *Resources* section for the address). While an issue from last year won't have this year's dates, the addresses and other particulars may be of great help to those planning vacations, or hoping to tour the festivals as performers. The 1981 festival was held August 7 to 9, which gives you an idea of the time of year it takes place. A book you might find helpful is *International Guide to Music Festivals*, by Douglas Smith and Nancy Barton (see the *Resources* section for address).

There are so many such festivals that the most recent attempt at a comprehensive listing (still by no means complete) contained over 1,500 entries. The best way to keep posted on the times and locations of festivals is to subscribe to one or more of the folk music periodicals listed in the *Resources* section. Generally the spring issue, or one of the early issues each year, will contain festival schedules.

One thing I've discovered from going to festivals is that there is usually so much going on at once that you can go crazy trying to take in everything you'd like to. Between workshops and several stages going at once, not to mention the parking-lot jam sessions, it becomes hard to choose. The best thing of all, though, is being around so many other

A parking lot jam session at the Tumwater Bluegrass Festival.

people who share your own love for music. It's like being at a big family reunion, and come to think of it, we really are all one big family.

If you do plan to attend a festival this season, the main advice is: Be prepared! Buy tickets in advance, bring warm clothes and rain gear, check out and reserve camping space or motel rooms in advance, and, most of all, be prepared to have a great time. Be sure to bring your instruments. Most folks agree that the parking-lot jam sessions are the highlight of any festival!

Song Section

Recorded versions of these songs are available through

King Noodle Records, Box 25,
Duvall, Washington 98019.

I Thought That I Was Broken

Marc Bris

so I was on the road an' two days out and I fin'lly got a chance to sleep
but when I woke up my guitar was gone ad so was all my eats

so I was out on the wrong end of Billings, Montana, tryin' to catch a ride to go
and it was mighty cold, I had nothin' left, and then it started to snow

but did I lose heart at the end of the line, did I kneel down and pray?
no I thought that I was broken so I threw myself away

(chorus)

well a cop come along and I was standin' there and he already knew my name
he said "I got some of your stuff at the station you can come down and claim"

and then he took me on out to the other end of town it was a bright sunshiney day
and my guitar was back, so was my food so I sat right down to play

(chorus)

Blue Guitar Pick

Marc Bristol

string them ol' beads that I found in the dirt
and I'm savin' all my appleseeds, too
and I can string a few words on an old melody
and make a song and I can sing it for you
well, I like things that you find for free
things that I see that I know are for me
I like things that you find for free
keep your eyes open and you'll see what I mean

Cabin in the Woods

Marc Bristol

seein' folks and family from the mountain top on down
livin' up in the pine trees and way down, down in the dirty old town

(chorus, no words: F F G G7 C)

but when we drove down that ol' two track road 'til we couldn't drive no more
had to walk to get to your door I knew it sure would feel like home

home is where your heart is, I know
cause I've been down that road so many, many times before

(chorus)

but I know it sure feels good to warm this heart in a cabin in the woods

headed down that road to home with plenty of sights to see
sleepin' in our van at night, sometimes I know that we're part gypsy

we been down to Disney land and we've been for a ride
but nothin' beats the pretty scene of the moonlight on the snow covered mountainside

(chorus)

and just a little cabin in the woods but you know it sure does feel like home
just a little cabin in the woods but you know it sure does feel like home.

My Lady

Marc Bristol

my lady makes me feel just like some music
I write a song each time I see her face
and she's gonna visit in the mountains where I live
we'll sit beside a mountain stream
and I will sing my song for her again

(repeat first verse)

You're Already There

Marc Bris

C F
I spent a quiet summer by the road side

G7 C
I wasn't thinkin' what I had to do bu

F
you're so bus y thinkin' bout to mor row I

G7 C
guess to day's not good e nough for you but

F
now I'm livin' in a cabin in the mountains I got

G7 C
old wood stove and it leaks a little smoke I got

F
dog named Molly by my side there's a lotta things that I

G7 C
haven't tried I'm learnin' just how much I've got to learn

well, sometimes I get lonesome in the mountains
but not as much as down there in the smoke
yes and I could use some company
so come on up and play with me
or stay down in the city there and choke

sometimes I feel just like a coin in your collection
I'm looked at once or twice and put away
but don't you think it's gonna be your luck
you'll try to spend me and I'll get stuck
in a vendin' machine on some ol' rainy day
(repeating chords & approximate melody of last line)
and the coca cola company won't pay

(chorus)

write you down a new song every day
and when you get done singin' 'em, throw 'em all away
but I'm writin' down this song for you
so you'll know I've got something to do
and I'll get fed when mealtime comes around
but I get food stamps now just once a month
I go down and I tell 'em what I do
well, I'm sittin' high up on the mountain
helpin' mother nature throwin' rocks down into silver creek below
this ole mountain one day got to go

(chorus)

(the tempo slows quite a bit for this last half verse)
well, once I used to think that I was jesus
and I'd be the one to come and save the day
but it looks like all my sad songs are behind me
come on molly, let's go out and play
guess I've collected enough rocks for today

Goin' Down To The River

(This blues is a typical example of the sort of song you can easily make up your own verses for. Go down to the river and try making up some of your rhymed couplets to go with these. By the way, this is easier to sing than it is to read or write. Blues comes from an aural tradition, after all. Because of the rocking tempo you'll find some quarter notes divided into three equal parts, designated as eighth notes.)

Music traditional. Lyrics by Marc Bri

I'll take my kids to the river, take off their shoes
let 'em run in the mud — we're gonna lose these blues
I'm goin' down to the river, set in the sun
watch the water flowin' by and let my mind run

I'm goin' down to the river, take my ol' guitar
gonna write you a new song wherever you are
I'm goin' down to the river, set in the sun
watch the water flowin' by and let my mind run

I'm goin' down to the river, gonna set in the sand
might stay all night and join the bullfrog band
I'm goin' down to the river, set in the sun
hear the music flowin' by and let my mind run

I'm goin' down to the river, feel that sweet, cool breeze
just gonna lay there on my back and look up at the trees
I'm goin' down to the river, set in the sun
watch the clouds floatin' by and let my mind run

Leave Your Cares Behind

Marc Bristol

have faith my friend and understand when you are on the road
that now's the time for reaping all the seeds that you have sowed
and what's really going on is never hidden by a code
and I pray that our good feelings help to lighten up your load

please don't think unkindly of the rest of us at home
we've found what we are looking for and have no need to roam
I don't know if there's any consolation in a poem
but I pray that if it gets too rough you'll know the way back home

take good care you're leaving and leave all your cares behind
set out on the open road and see what you can find
some day you might settle down, and maybe then you'll see
that all your little problems are not really caused by me

This Feelin'

Marc Bris

seems like it's been ages since I've been down to the river
I went down to Buffalo to learn to sing the blues
but the present is a gift that lasts forever and for always
and you believe in what you're doin' or it just won't feel like home

(refrain)

I am just so glad that there is something I can give you
springtime in my heart and I am writing songs again
all I really needed was a place that I could live at
the good lord knows that I've got country music in my soul

(refrain)

Magic Words

Marc Bristol

seems like we all have a few magic words
that light up the fire inside
if you tell me 'bout your favorite thing
maybe I can take you for a ride

'Cause I like to sing about favorite things
and I like to sing all night long
with my guitar in hand, and a few magic words
I can turn my life into a song

some of us like a good love song
some want to boogie all night
some of us need to hear a song about leaving
or staying 'til the morning's first light
some of us like them ol' songs about moonshine
some think the sunshine is best
if you tell me 'bout your favorite thing
I'll take care of the rest

(refrain and repeat first half of first verse)

BANJO CHORDS IN C TUNING

The little circle above a string indicates a string played open. An x above the string means the string is not played, or is deadened. In the banjo chord section, the circle and line on the left of the diagram indicates that the fifth string is played open. The fifth string is not used for all chords. Various methods are used to capo the fifth string to facilitate playing in other keys.

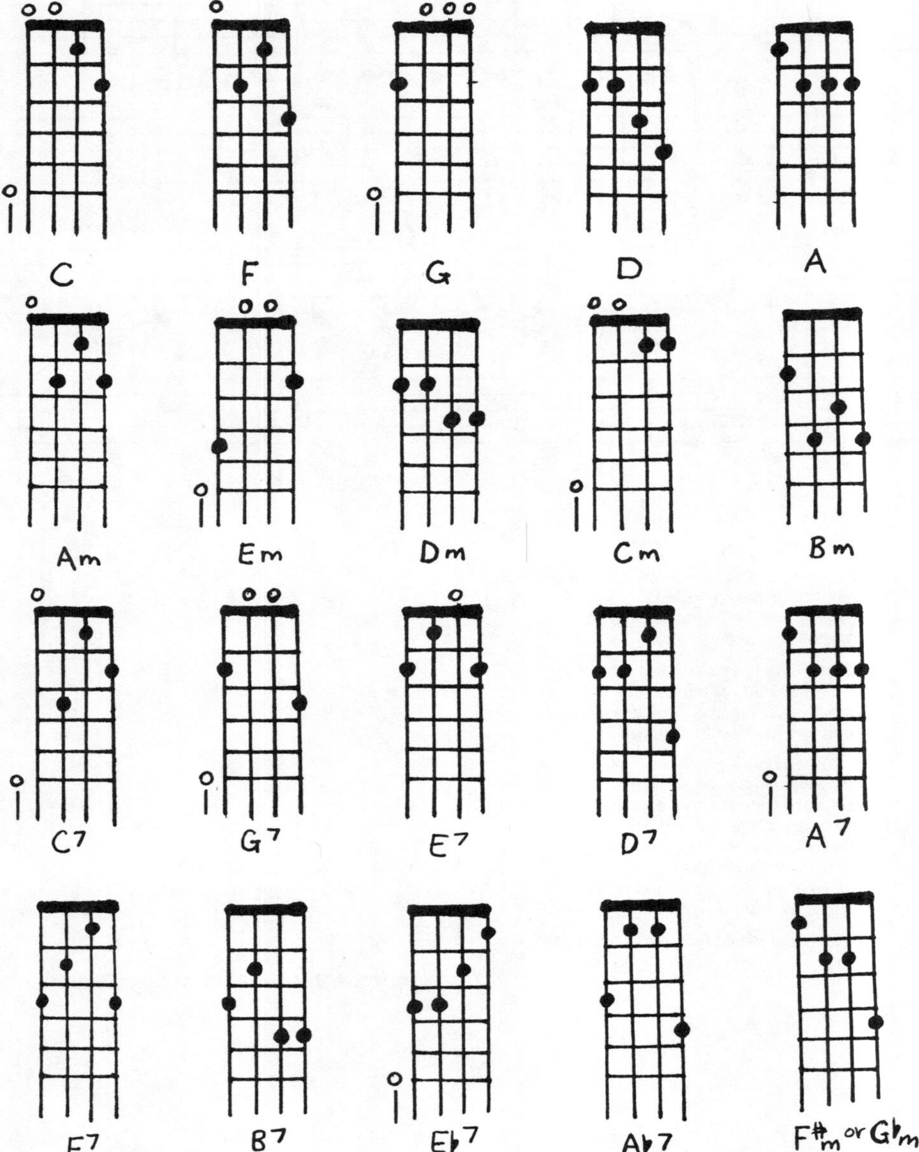

C tuning is G C G B D, with the B here being just below middle C on a piano. The high G is tuned to the note at the D string's fifth fret. Any chord form where all four long strings are fretted can be moved up the neck to make other chords, but the fifth or high string is not played — only when the note sounds good in the chord. These chords are also used in plectrum banjo, which is tuned the same but lacks the fifth string. (The A7 here is an exception; for plectrum banjo play the G string open to get A7 with the rest of this fingering.)

BANJO CHORDS IN G TUNING

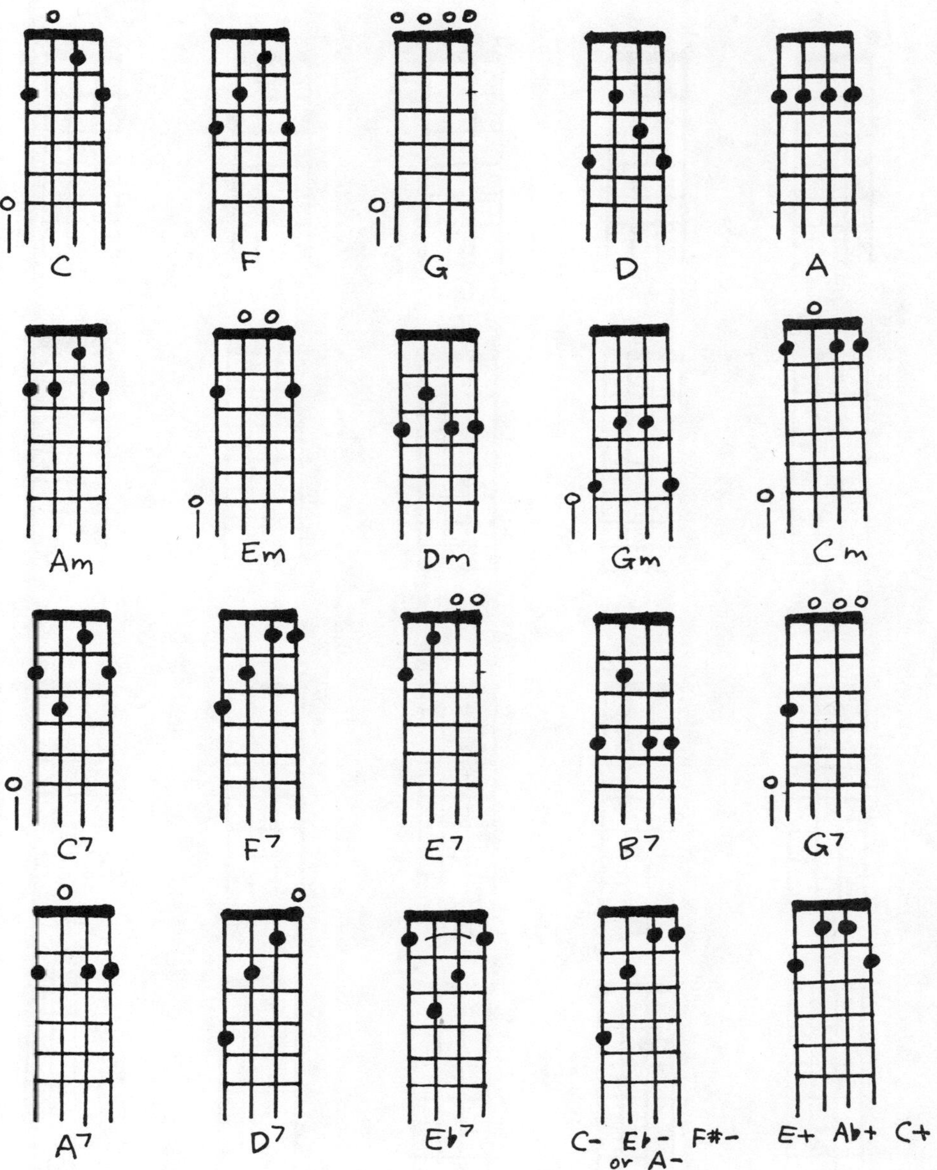

G tuning is nearly the same as C tuning, but the C string is tuned up to D, forming an open G chord. This tuning is used by most bluegrass banjo players, including Jonathan Schneider, who plays on my album. There are a wide variety of other chords available, and these charts are intended just to get you started. All the chords used in the songs in this book are shown here, plus some extras. I use a variation of the same fingerpick pattern shown in the guitar-playing section to play banjo, and favor C tuning. For other styles and chords, there are plenty of books available, some with records to hear what you're trying to play.

MANDOLIN CHORDS

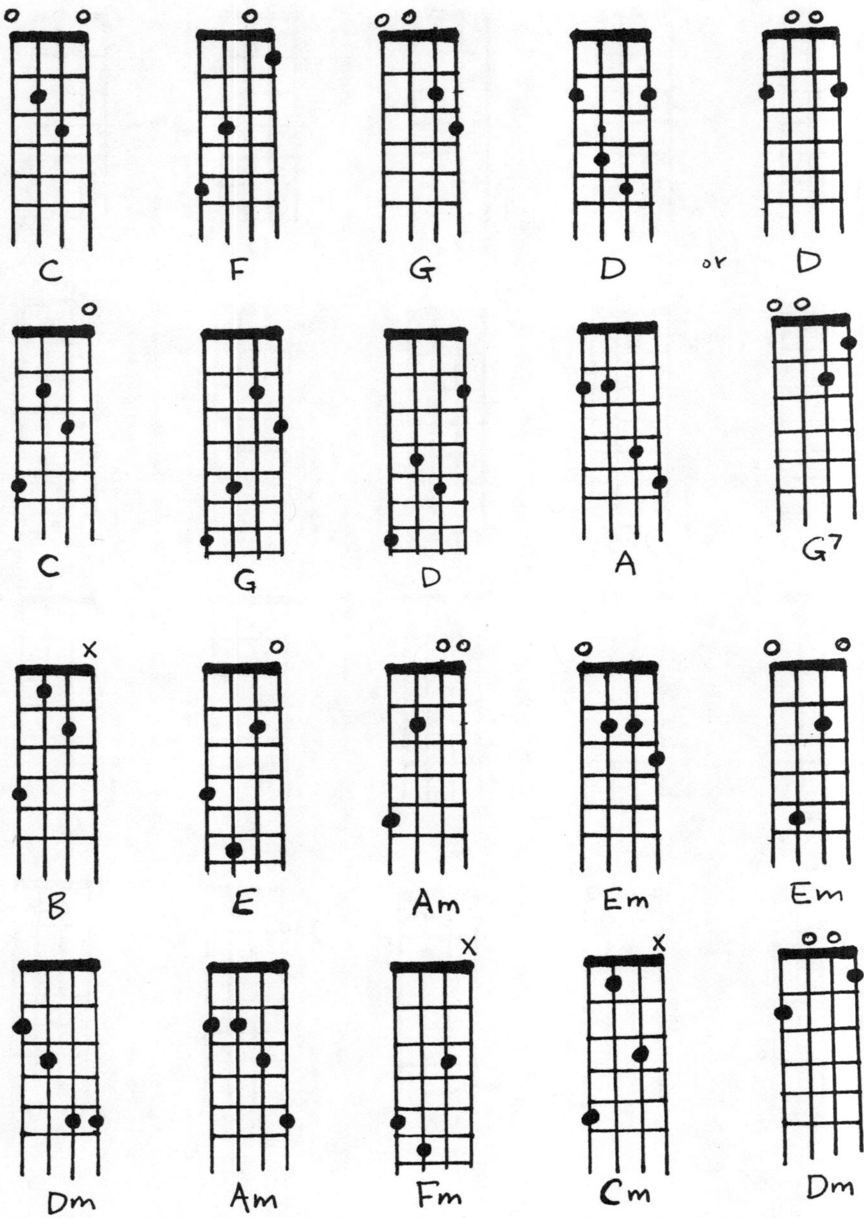

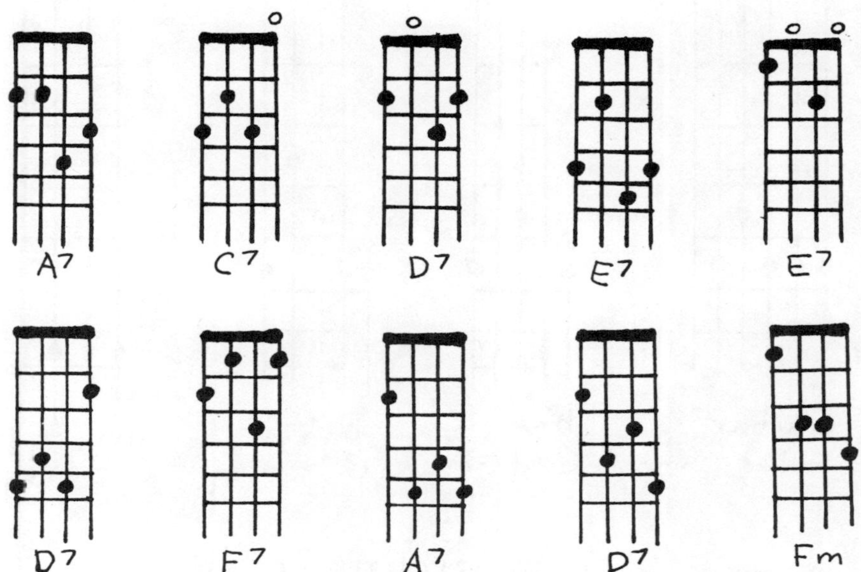

A mandolin is tuned the same as a fiddle — G D A E. Starting with the lowest pair, higher strings can be tuned to the note found at the seventh fret. As with the banjo chords, the forms here with all four strings fretted can be moved up the neck to obtain other chords. Additionally, I've included some three-string chords. A full chord only needs three notes (for major chords, minor chords only), so these fingerings can also be moved around. I've also included some simple chord fingerings for beginners. When you advance a bit you'll find that you may want those four string fingerings so you can chop off the chord (by lifting your fingers a bit to deaden the strings) to get a good "chunk." Chunk is the word used to describe the mandolin rhythm lick used in most bluegrass backup.

Since the string pairs are tuned in unison and fingered as one, my diagrams indicate them as one string.

While most banjo playing is done around chord fingerings, using hammer-ons and pull-offs (as described in the section in Chapter 4 on guitar playing), mandolin players play a lot of single note lines, and two note chord fragments while taking breaks. So below I'm indicating a bit of scale information on a diagram of a mandolin neck.

Besides the chunk rhythm lick, another technique used widely in mandolin backup and lead work is called tremoloing. Tremoloing consists of a rapid, regular (rhythmically) picking of a single note, or sometimes a two-note chord fragment. Both of these techniques can be heard on my album.

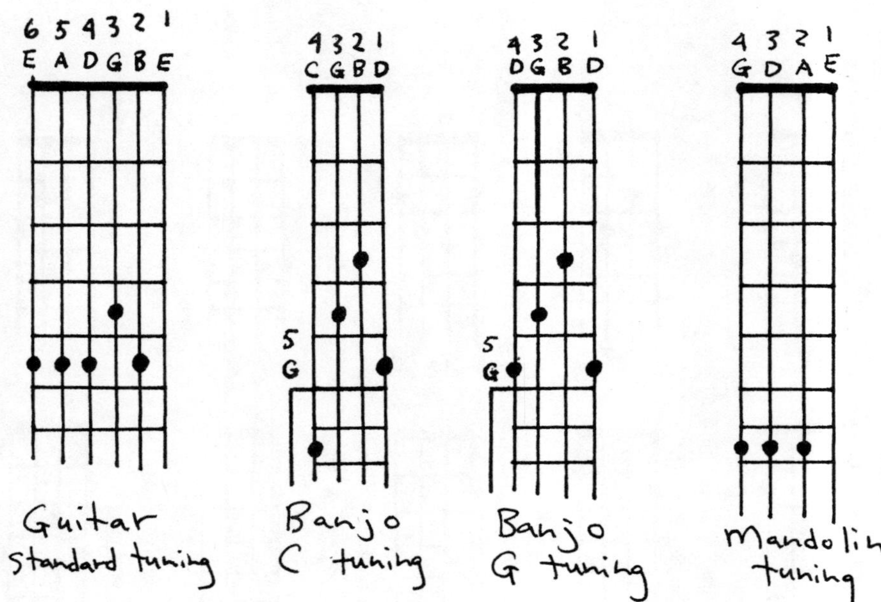

SYSTEMS FOR TUNING GUITAR, BANJO AND MANDOLIN

In the above tuning systems, the fret positions indicated by the dots give the note for the next string higher in pitch (the one to the right except in the case of the banjo fifth string. The note on the first string at the fifth fret is for the fifth string.) The numbering system may seem confusing, since the numbers go up while the pitch goes down. I don't know why it's that way, but this is traditional, and you'll find the strings numbered this way in the packages when you buy them.

The G string on the guitar can be used as a starting point for both banjo and mandolin.

DULCIMER CHORDS — MODAL SCALES

Since the dulcimer neck and dulcimer tunings (for an Appalachian dulcimer, that is) lend themselves well to a discussion of modal scales, I'm going to use them to explain that concept. One reason the dulcimer is considered easy to play is the fact that there are no "extra" frets — the notes along the melody string are all in the scale you'll be using for your melody. If you look at my fretboard diagrams (or at your own dulcimer if you have one), you'll see that all the fret spacings are not equal. On a chromatic instrument such as a guitar, the fret spacings gradually diminish to compensate for less pitch change as the string is depressed more towards the middle. There are twelve tones in a chromatic scale (in half-step increments), but we use an eight-tone scale in most Western music. The most common *mode* used in our music (the standard do-re-mi scale) is called the Ionian mode. On a guitar, each fret up the neck creates what we call a half-step change in pitch, and two frets distance is a whole step.

On the dulcimer, the longer spaces are whole steps, and the shorter ones are half steps. The spacing of notes in the Ionian scale then, are: 1-1-½-1-1-1-½. Changing the order of the spacing by starting in a different spot creates a different mode. For example, the Dorian mode spacings are: 1-½-1-1-1-½-1. The names of the modes in order (the last step or half step takes you up to the same note an octave, or eight tones, higher) are: Ionian, Dorian, Phrygian, Lydian, Myxolydian, Aeolian, and Locrian. For each modal system, add the first number of the previous system to the end of the line and you obtain the correct note spacings.

What we call a minor scale (a variation of which is used in the guitar blues pattern chart) is the Aeolian mode. Other possibilities are available on chromatic instruments. A scale I enjoy using for a Mideastern sound (belly dancing music, etc.) has these spacings: ½-1½-½-1-½-1½-½ (notice the symmetry).

So here are some chord diagrams for the dulcimer in a couple of the more commonly-used tunings, the Ionian and the Myxolydian. Mark Filler prepared these diagrams, and he plays dulcimer on the recorded version of "Mountain Lullaby." Mark used the Myxolydian tuning on the recording, and played one of the C chords where I played F in the final section.

What I am calling the "melody" string (the one the scale goes along) is the lowest one in these diagrams.

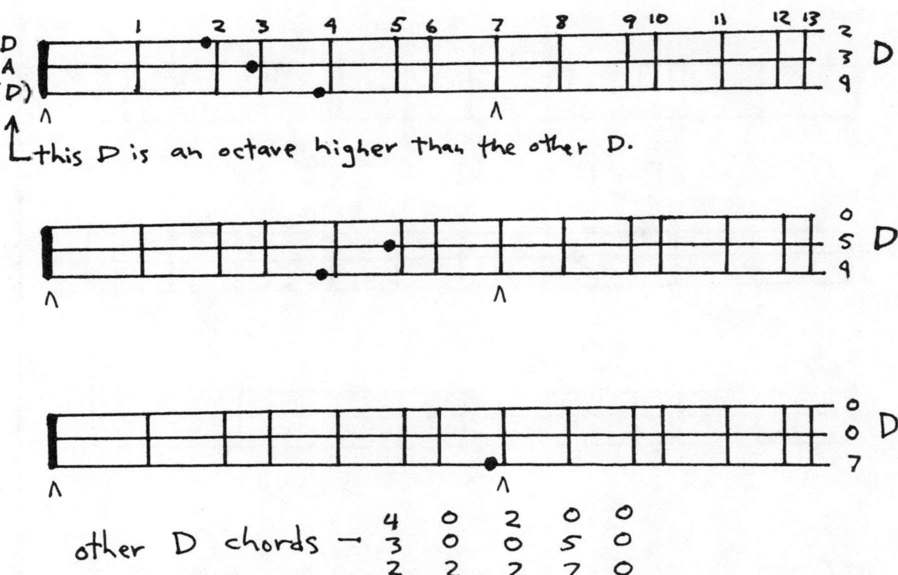

These are D chords in the Myxolydian tuning. (The tuning is indicated to the left of the first diagram.) As you can see, there are several different ways to play a D chord. These are called different "voicings." The chord sounds a little different in each one, and you can use whichever one sounds best as a backup for the melody you are singing.

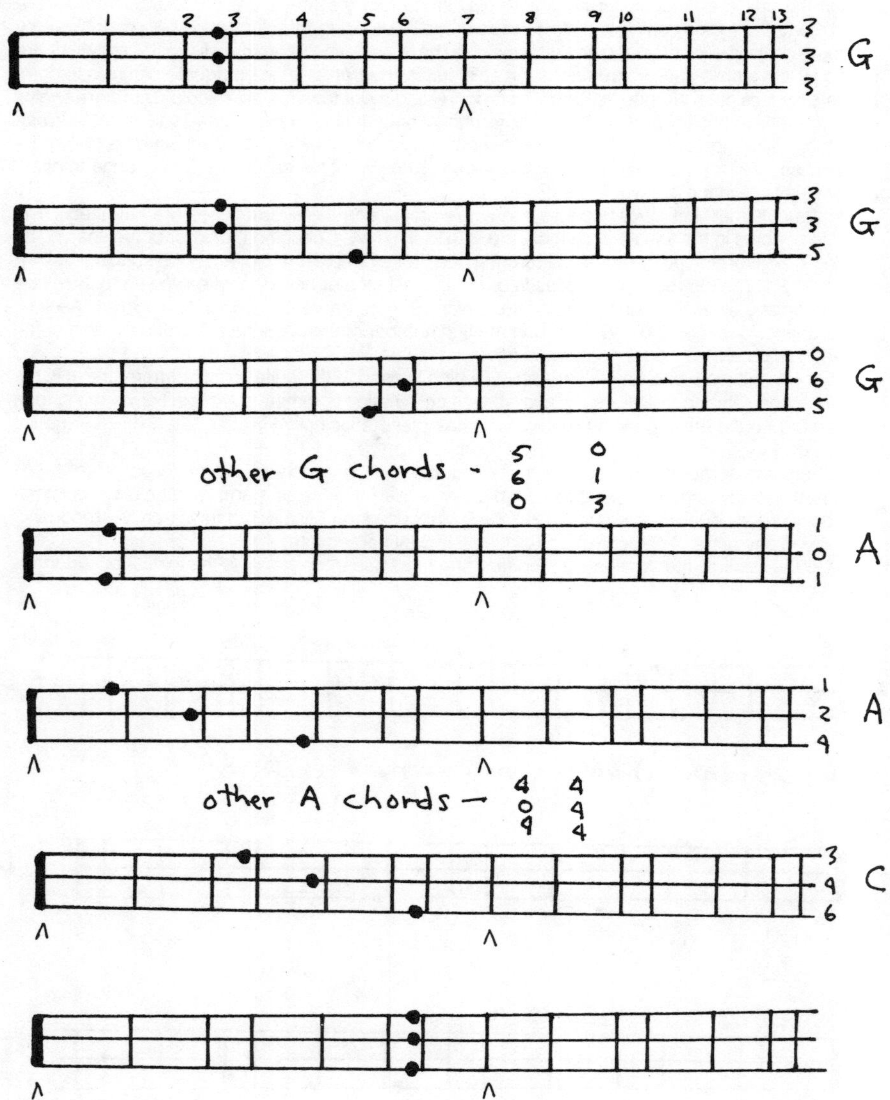

Chords in Myxolydian tuning—key of D. The scale goes from the open string to the 7th fret, where it repeats.

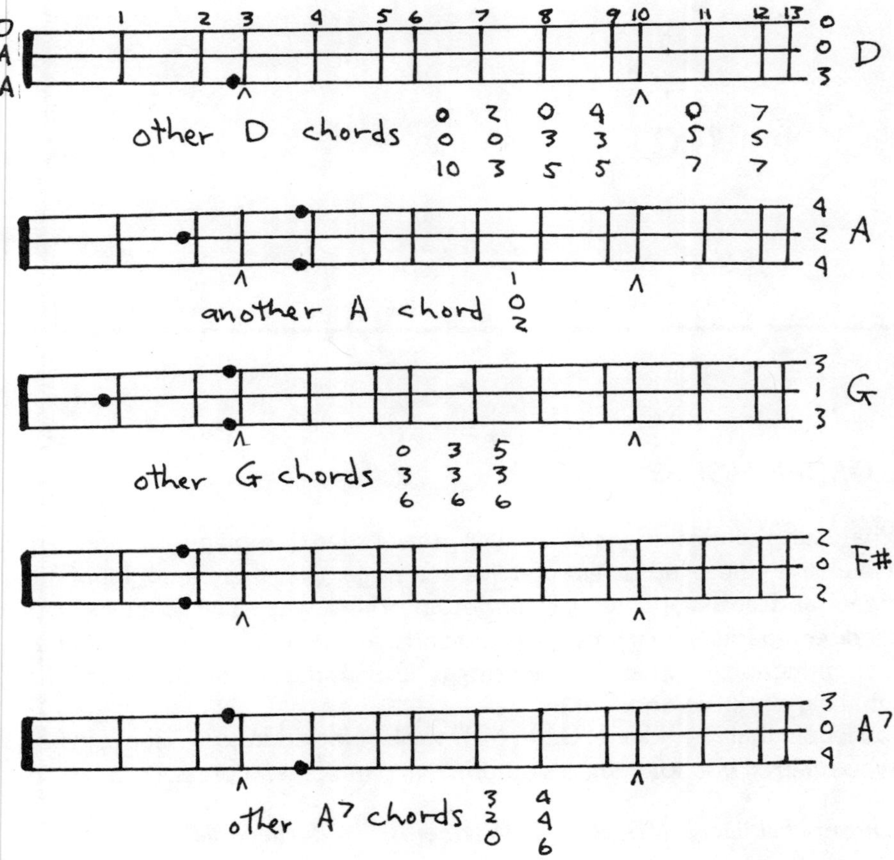

These chords are for the Ionian tuning, key of D. (The tuning is indicated to the left of the first diagram.) The scale goes from the 3rd fret to the 10th fret. This tuning would be used when you needed to use melody notes below your lowest tonic note (which on the melody string is at the 3rd fret). There are, of course, many possibilities other than those I've shown here. There are a few books available which cover some of these possibilities—a particularly good one is *In Search of the Wild Dulcimer*, by Force and d'Ossche (available from several of the mail order suppliers listed in the *Resources* section).

Resources

MAIL-ORDER HOUSES

What with the cost of gas these days, mail-order shopping gets more and more attractive all the time. And unless you live in a major city, there are a lot of folk music instruments and accessories you can't get any other way. The following mail-order merchandisers specialize in things like banjo parts, luthier tools, instruction manuals, and even such mundane things as dulcimer strings. Usually the cost is lower than what you'd pay in that big-city store, too.

You'll note that I've added "Dept. MB" to all of the addresses—that's just so they'll know who referred you to them. It's an optional part of the address.

Andy's Front Hall, Dept. MB, R.D. 1, Wormer Rd., Voorheesvile, NY 12186

Front Hall started as a record company, with a hammered dulcimer album recorded by Andy's husband, Bill. He has since then made more albums, and the folks have thoughtfully added several books, instruments, accessories, and records on other labels to their catalog, which you can obtain free for the asking. (Dulcimer kits are available from Andy's.)

Backyard Music, Dept. MB, 509 S. 44th St., Philadelphia, PA 19104

David Cross, the man behind Backyard Music, has designed a dulcimer kit that can be put together by a third grader. In fact, he designed the kit for the third graders he teaches. Dave sent me a finished Backyard Music dulcimer (at the recommendation of Maddy MacNeil, editor of *Dulcimer Player's News*—see the folk music publications section of *Resources* for the address) and I am real impressed with it. Everyone I know who plays dulcimer is quite skeptical about it when I tell them it's made of cardboard—some so much so that they fail to see the beauty of it!

After all, many of the greatest guitar players known started by building a cigar-box model when they were young. This cardboard instrument sounds great! Except for the guitar tuners, the design of this kit is basically what you might find some fellow way back in the hills making out of what he could scrounge. (The total homegrown model might have carved tuning pegs.) The body is ordinary 200-pound-test corrugated cardboard. The neck is one-by-two. Head and tail blocks are made from small chunks of two-by-four. The frets are finishing nails, bent 90 degrees at the tip and driven into holes at the end of a saw-cut slot at each fret position. The bridge and nut are fashioned from pieces of thick masonite.

Guitar-tuning machines are not real hard to scrounge, either. David has put together a booklet describing his design for those who would like to build their own from scratch—*Make Your Own Dulcimer Using Common Materials*. Of course his kits come with instructions, too, and if you purchase six or more kits you also get a pamphlet titled *Groups Building Dulcimers* (which is also available separately). Finished cardboard dulcimers round out the lineup, together with kits. This is real homegrown stuff!

Black Mountain Instruments, Dept. MB, 16264 Main St., P.O. Box 779, Lower Lake, CA 95457

These folks make a line of wood dulcimer kits, with mahogany, cherry, or walnut sides and back, and spruce tops. They've been known to give special deals to "Homegrown Music" readers, so mention that you are one if you write.

Charlie Blacklock, Dept. MB, 1821 Saint Charles St., Alameda, CA 94501.

Charlie sells musical saws.

Blue Ridge Dulcimer Shop, Dept. MB, P.O. Box 2164, Winchester, VA 22601

These are the same folks who publish *Dulcimer Player's News* (listed in the folk music section of *Resources*). As you can imagine, the focus here is on dulcimers (both the Appalachian and the hammered variety), kits, books, records, and accessories.

Buckhorn Mountain Woodcrafts, Dept. MB, 465 Buckhorn Mountain Rd., Winlock, WA 98596

This is a craft house that sells box drums. Write for a catalog.

Capritaurus, Dept. MB, P.O. Box 153, Felton, CA 95018

These folks deal with that devilish habit things have of fluctuating in price by publishing a loose-leaf catalog and issuing a series of supplements, with additions and corrections to the original catalog. Instruments, kits, records, books, and accessories are featured. Instrument-building accessories and tools are found in the Capritaurus catalog, with one color photograph of completed dulcimers made from their kits, which were the take-off point for this whole operation. These folks also operate a store and instrument-building shop.

Dusty Strings Dulcimer Co., Dept. MB, 1848 NE Ravenna Blvd., Seattle, WA 98105

These folks offer kits for two styles of hammered dulcimers, a single-bridge and a double-bridge instrument. The kits are available in "just-sand-it-and-finish-it" form, and with a variety of woods and fancy details.

Elderly Instruments, Dept. MB, 541 E. Grand River, P.O. Box 1795, East Lansing, MI 48823-6795

These folks offer about the most extensive stringed instrument catalog that I know of. Their free catalog even contains some information sections, such as one on how to mount a skin head on a banjo and another on where to find folk music publications. The catalog also has such things as harmonicas, recorders, *kalimbas* (African thumb pianos), and so forth. They offer books and records both for instruction and entertainment, along with parts and tools for instrument building. By all means order the catalog. Orders are filled promptly.

Elderly also publishes a newsletter listing used instruments for sale, and somebody there can give you an idea of what yours is worth if you're thinking of selling. The company operates a store and an instrument repair shop as well as a catalog sales department.

The Fiddle Works, Dept. MB, P.O. Box 1250, MacLean, VA 22101

These folks produce a real homegrown-style fiddle kit. The body of the instrument is band sawed and hollowed out from a two-by-eight. The top is pine, and the tailpiece is a bent table fork! If you like funky charm, and that real down-home style, this is one place to find it.

Guitar's Friend, Dept. MB, Rt. 1, Box 200, Sandpoint, ID 83864

Handmade instruments seem to be the first love of these folks who build their own. Their catalog is similar to Elderly's. Because of price fluctuations, both outfits publish separate price lists. The difference is that Guitar's Friend asks for $3.65 before they'll send you the lavishly illustrated catalog. With the price list, you do receive brochures on the handmade instruments, however. This outfit has a store as well as a catalog-sales department.

Gurian Guitars, Ltd., Dept. MB, Box 595, West Swanzey, NH 03469

Instrument-building materials (some of which are pre-formed), tools, and accessories are the long and short of Gurian's bill of fare. This company is one of the main sources for woods, hardware, and finishing materials used by luthiers everywhere. Besides parts for acoustic instruments, you'll find pickups, and various other parts for electric instruments.

Handverks, Dept. MB, Hwy. 57, Sister Bay, WI 52434

Ocarinas and instructional materials.

Hobgoblin Music, Dept. MB, P.O. Box 5311, South San Francisco, CA 94080

Vintage concertinas and other unusual new, used, and vintage instruments are sold here. Records and books, too.

Homespun Tapes, Dept. MB, Box 694, Woodstock, NY 12498

Instructional materials for guitar, banjo, and other instruments.

Hum Drums, Dept. MB, 2321-B Roosevelt, Berkeley, CA 94073

This is a craft house that sells box drums. Write for a catalog.

International Luthier's Supply, Dept. MB, P.O. Box 1544, Tulsa, OK 74112

More instrument-building materials, tools, accessories, and instructions. In each category you'll find some items that you won't find anywhere else. These folks have kits and parts for a wide variety of instruments—stringed mostly—but including an African thumb piano kit. The catalog is called the "Bowed and Fretted Instrument Catalog," and you'll find plenty of violin kits and parts here.

Jean's Dulcimer Shop, Dept. MB, P.O. Box 8, Cosby, TN 37722

You guessed it—dulcimers. These folks (at the Folk Life Center of the Smokies) also produce records and hold festivals.

Joe & Nancy Kasik, Dept. MB, 147 Tatum Lane, Eugene, OR 94704

Bamboo flutes.

Lark in the Morning, Dept. MB, Box 1176, Mendocino, CA 95460

Celtic and other ethnic instruments can be found here.

Legacy Books, Dept. MB, Box 494, Hatboro, PA 19040

A source for all types of folklore, including music. Also folk history, anthroplogy, and so forth. Ask here for out-of-print titles. You can subscribe to the newsletter and be kept up to date on new books on these subjects.

Hank Levin, Dept. MB, Box 1882, Everett, WA 98206

Hank and his wife, Lynn, have been making dulcimers for quite some time. They formerly owned a company called Musical Traditions, whose product now is made in Sandpoint, Idaho, and is available through the Guitar's Friend catalog. When their current company was based in Los Angeles, they used the name Smoggy Mountain Dulcimers, but now that they've moved to the cleaner air of the Northwest (Everett?), all that has changed. Anyhow, these folks have just one kit design, so you can imagine that they've honed their act to a fine tune. The kit is called the "Tennessee Teardrop" and is made from cherry wood. The kit price includes instructions and *glue.*

Monty Levenson, Dept. MB, P.O. Box 294, Willits, CA

Shakuhachi flutes, related books.

The Luthier's Mercantile, Dept. MB, Box 774, 412 Moore Lane, Healdsburg, CA 95448

Luthier tools and supplies.

Mandolin Brothers, Ltd., Dept. MB, 629 Forest Ave., Staten Island, NY 10310

New and old instruments.

Metropolitan Music Co., Dept. MB, Mountain Road R.D. 1, Stowe, VT 05672

Luthier supplies.

Musician's Supply, Dept. MB, P.O. Box 1440, El Cajon, CA 92020

Electric guitarists are the focus of this outfit's catalog, though some acoustic guitars are featured, and instructional material deals with all types of guitar playing, plus a little on banjo playing. Discount prices are the name of the game, and in recent years the selection has narrowed in the interest of high-volume sales. Sound-reinforcement equipment and accessories are to be found, at up to 40 percent off the list price. I don't like to buy that sort of stuff without trying it out first, but if you have a store nearby that carries the same stuff, and your store won't match the price (or come close after you pay freight costs), by all means order from the catalog. Quality is guaranteed. These guys claim to ship orders the same day they receive them, and many items can be ordered by phone at a toll-free number. Service is good; I've tried it.

Music Sales Corporation, Dept. MB, P.O. Box 572, 5 Bellevale Road, Tester, NY 10918

This is a mail-order book company, featuring books published by Oak Publications. By far the largest producer of folk music instruction books, Oak has several fascinating articles in its catalog. Though many of these books are available through the other catalogs mentioned here, none of the others offer the complete line, nor do they have as full descriptions of the books in most cases.

Mussehl & Westphal, Dept. MB, 130, Delevan, WI 53115

Makers of the Professional Musical Saw. You can order just the saw and case, or the whole kit, which includes instructions, string bow and dowel bow, rosin, and striker. These folks occasionally publish a newsletter called *Sawing News of the World*, the most recent edition of which you get with an order.

Natural Music, Dept. MB, Route D, Marblemount, WA 98267

Mostly strings and accessories.

Spirited Woodworking/Lunar Rhythms, Dept. MB, 21355 Hwy. 20 E., Bend, OR 97701

Wooden spoons, rhythm sticks, tambourines, tongue drums and other percussion instruments.

Stewart-MacDonald, Dept. MB, Box 900, Athens, OH 45701

Banjo kits, accessories, and tools are the take-off point for this outfit, though some books are also included in the catalog.

String Instrument Service, Dept. MB, 597 Wellfleet Dr., Bay Village, OH 44140

Similar fare to Gurian's, but featuring guitar-making kits.

Vikwood Limited, Dept. MB, Box 554, 1221A Superior Avenue, Sheboygan, WI 53081

Wood for building guitars.

Vitali Import Company, Dept. MB, 5944 Atlantic Blvd., Maywood, CA 90270

These folks carry instrument-building materials as well as dulcimer kits. Particularly notable is their book selection, which features several titles I'm sure you'd have quite a hard time finding anywhere else. These books deal primarily with instrument building, both stringed and wind.

FOLK MUSIC PUBLICATIONS

Folk music magazines are full of useful information. You'll find advertisements for kits and other mail-order products as well as articles about performers, instrument builders and the music itself. In addition, these magazines are the only really good source of folk music festival schedules. Many new festivals are started each year, and the only way to find out about them is through the periodicals.

Thanks go to Elderly Instruments Catalog, *The Victory Music Folk & Jazz Review*, and *Come for to Sing* for invaluable aid in compiling this listing. Apologies go to all the regional publications escaping mention here. Let me know about your magazine or newsletter and I'll surely mention it in my column in *The Mother Earth News*.

Banjo Newsletter, Dept. MB, 1310 Hawkins Ln., Annapolis, MD 21401

I haven't seen this one, but it is recommended as a source of information on banjo playing and players.

Bluegrass Unlimited, Dept. MB, Box 111, Broad Run, VA 22014

You can guess what this one's about. It is the definitive source for bluegrass-festival scheduling as well as articles on the performers, instruments, books and records.

Come for to Sing, Dept. MB, 917 W. Wolfram, Chicago, IL 60657

The focus is on Chicago and the Midwest, but the articles and reviews are of interest to anyone who is into folk music. Calendar items are for local events, but the other material is universal, dealing with folk musicians and their music. There are columns on bluegrass and blues, many songs and interviews. There is an Annual Guide to Folk Music Resources in the first issue each year, and a Festival Guide in the Spring issue.

The Devil's Box, Dept. MB, Route 4, Madison, AL 35758

A fiddling quarterly published by the Tennessee Valley Old Time Fiddler's Association. It has articles, tablatures, record reviews, and so forth.

Dulcimer Player's News, Dept. MB, P.O. Box 2164, Winchester, VA 22601

This publication has information on both types of dulcimers, plus players, songs, techniques, builders, and book and record reviews. I recommend this to the total dulcimer nut.

Festival of the Saws, c/o KUSP, P.O. Box 423, Santa Cruz, CA 95061

This newsletter has information on the annual musical saw festival in Santa Cruz, California. Send a stamped, self-addressed envelope with your request.

The Fiddle Works Calendar, P.O. Box 1250, MacLean, VA 22101

This publication has listings of events featuring fiddle playing and folk music in general. These folks also produce the fiddle kit, mentioned in the mail-order section of *Resources*, and they've recently started carrying albums for sale by mail.

Folkscene, Dept. MB, P.O. Box 64545, Los Angeles, CA 90064

This publication gives information about West Coast folk music.

Frets, Dept. MB, 20605 Lazaneo, Cupertino, CA 95014

This is a comprehensive magazine, with regular columns by acknowledged experts on several popular instruments, as well as repair and construction techniques. There are feature articles on famous players and instrument builders. Regular columnists are Mike Auldridge (dobro), Alan Munde (banjo), Byron Berline (fiddle), Dan Crary (flat-pick guitar), David Grisman (mandolin), and several others.

Golden West Bluegrass, Dept. MB, P.O. Box 341, Bonsall, CA 92003

You'll find features on groups and individual players—clogging too! Also festival notes and schedules (of course), playing tips, and record and book reviews.

Grass Clippings, Dept. MB, 1437 W. Howard St., Chicago, IL 60626

This is the newsletter of the Chigago Area Bluegrass Music and Pickin' Society (C.A.B.M.A.P.S.). It contains regional schedules. The society meets at the scene of festivals.

Guild of American Luthiers Quarterly, Dept. MB, 8222 S. Park, Tacoma, WA 98408

A subscription comes with membership in the guild, and includes the data sheet series. Articles are written by members of the organization, which holds a yearly convention, surely an exciting event for anyone involved in instrument building. The amount and quality of information available through the Guild is tremendous. I recommend this magazine highly.

Guitar & Mandonlin, Dept. MB, 1600 Billman Ln., Silver Springs, MD 20902

This one comes out six times a year, with playing tips, articles, reviews, interviews, and so forth.

Guitar Player, Dept. MB, 20605 Lazaneo, Cupertino, CA 95014

This magazine is published by the folks who publish *Frets*, with a different editor and writers but a similar format, devoted just to guitar and electric bass. You'll find product reviews, interviews, and regular columns on several styles of guitar playing.

Hey Rube!, Dept. MB, P.O. Box 9693, Minneapolis, MN 55440

An organization for professional folk artists (performers), featuring gig lists and group health insurance; also a newsletter.

International Banjo, Dept. MB, P.O. 328, Kissimee, FL 32741

This publication focuses on banjo styles, and not just bluegrass banjo or even just five-string banjo—the whole works, tenor and plectrum included. Presumably these folks will eventually also cover banjo ukes and various other permutations of the instrument. It's a nice magazine.

Jazz String Newsletter, Dept. MB, P.O. Box 1513, Milwaukee, WI 53201

Designed as a forum for jazz string players (specifically, those instruments that are unfretted and bowed) to express themselves, this publication contains articles, interviews, transcriptions of tunes, and reviews of books and records, and will print whatever you might have to say on the subject!

JEMF Quarterly, Dept. MB, 11369 Bunche Hall, UCLA, Los Angeles, CA 90024

You'll find in-depth treatment of American traditional music here. A subscription includes membership in the Friends of the John Edwards Memorial Foundation.

Living Blues, Dept. MB, 2615 N. Wilton Ave., Chicago, IL 60614

This bi-monthly publication is devoted to the Black American Blues tradition. It has articles, interviews, concert schedules, and so forth.

Mandolin World News, Dept. MB, Box 2255, San Rafael, CA 94902

Tablature, playing tips, and articles on instruments and players are found here.

Musical Instrument Classified, 842 S. Monroe St., Arlington, VA 22204

This is just what it sounds like—thousands of ads for musical instruments for sale or trade.

National Council for the Traditional Arts Calendar, Dept. MB, 1346 Connecticut Ave. N.W., No. 1118, Washington, D.C. 20036

A calendar of folk festivals and related events, listing over 1,500 in the most recent edition. When ordering send S.A.S.E. Publication is sporadic.

North Country Folk, Dept. MB, Box 189, Ironwood, MI 49938

While this is another regional publication (quarterly), the content is often of wider interest. The issue I saw had an article on the musical saw by Dan Wallace, the owner of Mussehl & Westphal, makers of musical saws since 1921. Dan bought the company from Clarence Mussehl, and picked up plenty of saw-playing lore in the process.

Old Time Music, Dept. MB, 33 Brunswick Gardens, London, W8 4AW, England

Can you imagine an English magazine dedicated to American old-time country music? This is it (and it's not the only one either!). You'll find articles on well-known and obscure old timers in American rural music. Elderly Instruments recommends it highly.

OP, Dept. MB, P.O. Box 2391, Olympia, WA 98507

This magazine reviews all types of music, particularly rock and new wave, but I found an ad for a polka-music catalog in issue J. They reviewed my band's Western swing and rockabilly record, and did a good job! They will review your record if it is independently released. Distribution is nationwide, mainly to radio stations and other members of the music industry.

Resophonic Echoes, Dept. MB, R.R. 1, Madill, OK 73446

This publication covers all sorts of metal cone resonator guitars, and acoustic steel guitar playing, with interviews, playing tips, and more.

Sing Out!, Dept. MB, 270 Lafayette St., New York, NY 10012

This is the oldest folk music magazine around. Back issues from times like January 1966 are fascinating in their reporting of the furor over "folk rock." Bob Dylan had just played an electric guitar at the Newport Folk Festival when this issue came out. You'll find articles, songs, reviews, interviews, editorials, and Pete Seeger's "Johnny Appleseed Jr." column in this one.

Victory Music Folk & Jazz Review, Dept. MB, P.O. Box 36, Tillicum Br., Tacoma, WA 98492

This is another regional publication, serving the Puget Sound area in the Pacific Northwest. Calendar items are for local events, but record reviews are of wide interest. Feature articles tend to be on local performers. The magazine is distributed free locally in stores and clubs, and is available by mail for a small subscription price.

Walnut Valley Occasional, Dept. MB, Box 245, Winfield, KS 67156

This is a free publication, in tabloid format, designed to promote the National Guitar Flat-picking Championships at Winfield each summer, and various similar events held there at other times. It comes out about three times a year, and the record reviews alone make it worth your while, even if you have no intention of making it out to the festival.

Wisconsin Bluegrass News, Dept. MB, P.O. Box 64, Eagle River, WI 54521

This is a regional publication—with bluegrass festival schedules for the whole midwestern area, particularly Wisconsin, which apparently has a thriving bluegrass scene.

HOMEGROWN MUSIC ON RECORDS

The consumerist philosophy that regulates our throwaway culture dictates that we invent a new style of music every two or three years, so that everyone will need to run out and buy a new record library as well as a new wardrobe, car, and so forth. The large record companies, which dominate the market, tend to produce music aimed at a mass audience, with mass consciousness itself being the primary message in the music. As a result, cultural continuity and tradition suffer, and along with them individualism.

There are a good many smaller record companies, however, that are in business not so much to turn a profit as to make available a certain type of music. Most of them can't afford to advertise their products in the national media, nor can they depend on getting their specialized products distributed to stores everywhere. In larger cities, of course, there are usually stores that either carry some of these products or could at least order them for you. Other than selling the records directly off the stage at performances, though, the only truly effective way to market the independent-label record is through the mail.

I've compiled a list of independent folk music labels and distributors for independent labels here. By no means is it a complete list, and I encourage you to subscribe to *OP*, *Victory Music Folk & Jazz Review*, or one of the other specialty magazines listed in the folk music publications section of *Resources* for reviews of other companies' products.

Adelphi Records, Dept. MB, P.O. Box 288, Silver Spring, MD 20907

The East Coast folk music scene. Saul Broudy, Delaware Water Gap.

Arhoolie Records, Dept. MB, 10341 San Pablo Ave., El Cerrito, CA 94530

The blues, both country and city, make up a large portion of Arhoolie's large catalog. Many other styles are also represented, though, such as Cajun, Chicano (or Norteño), old-time country, gospel, contemporary folk, and even a little jazz. Arhoolie's biggest seller is Clifton Chenier, who plays zydeco music (essentially blues-rock sung in French, with accordian and scrub board the principle instruments).

Bay Records, Dept. MB, 1516 Oak St., Alameda, CA 94501

This label specializes in folk artists who either live in the San Francisco Bay area or are very popular there. Bluegrass, folk, old-time country, Irish, and other ethnic music. I highly recommend Hank Bradley's album, "Music of the Poison Coyote Kid," and "Gypsy Gyppo String Band" (by the band of the same name).

Biscuit City Records, Dept. MB, 3974 Waterhouse Rd., Oakland, CA 94602

This started as a Denver, Colorado-based label putting out all kinds of folk and old-time country music. I particularly recommend the earlier titles by the Ophelia Swing Band, if they are still in print. The new direction of the company is toward women making music, with acts like Rosy's Bar & Grill, Cathy Barton, and Marie Rhines.

County Records, Dept. MB, P.O. Box 191, Floyd, VA 24091

This label specializes in bluegrass and old-time country music, with both contemporary recordings and reissues of old-time artists. Buck White, Kenny Baker, Stanley Brothers, Norman Blake, and many, many others. The catalog is a must for bluegrass aficionados.

Down Home Music Company, Dept. MB, 10341 San Pablo Ave., El Cerrito, CA 94530

This major distributor for nearly every independent label with several releases has so large a selection of every type of folk music that it publishes a separate catalog for each type: Old-time country, rockabilly, bluegrass, Cajun, Irish, blues—you name it, they've got it!

Educational Activities, Dept. MB, Freeport, NY 11520

Records and other material for young children.

Folk Recordings, Dept. MB, the Library of Congress, Music Division, Recorded Sound Section, Washington, DC 20540

Several albums of traditional American music and its derivative forms are available. These have been compiled from the collections in the Archives of Folk Song. I haven't heard them, but included in the catalog (free for the asking) are several titles featuring American Indian songs and chants. These must be fascinating collections.

Flying Fish Records, Dept. MB, 1304 W. Schubert, Chicago, IL 60626

So many of these records are so great it's impossible to make a particular recommendation. These folks specialize in touring folk entertainers you will find at the major folk festivals. All the records are of very high quality, from performances and recording techniques to pressing and packaging. There is bluegrass (Hot Rize, Country Gazette, others), blues, folk, jazz, old-time country (Red Clay Ramblers, others), Irish, and other ethnic music. They also distribute a few other labels.

Henry the Fiddler, Dept. MB, 613 Michigan Ave., Evanston, IL 60202

Old-time fiddling live at a folk-festival jam session.

Kaliedoscope, Dept. MB, P.O. Box O, El Cerrito, CA 94530

This label made its fortune initially on the huge success of the David Grisman Quintet albums. David moved on to a major label, but Kaliedoscope has continued a fine tradition, with Kate Wolf joining the ranks and allowing her previously self-produced albums to be reissued on the Kaliedoscope label. There are also a couple of albums featuring Tiny Moore, the great swing mandolin player featured for years with Bob Wills's Texas Playboys.

Kicking Mule Records, Dept. MB, Box 158, Alderpoint, CA 95411

Although initially started as a label for solo blues guitarist Stephen Grossman, with the idea of producing records with accompanying instruction manuals, KMR has expanded to include many types of guitar music, a dulcimer series, and some banjo records—all with instruction tablature books available or soon to be. Many excellent choices. I particularly recommend George Gritzbach, who has two releases at this date.

Lone Oak Publications, Dept. MB, 1316 N. Edgemont, No. 309, Los Angeles, CA 90027

Relaxing cafe-mood guitar instrumentals.

Lone Tree Records, Dept. MB, 4748 S.E. Horstman Rd., Port Orchard, WA 98366

Music of the midwestern prairie, by Steve and Maureen (vocal duo, with guitar, banjo, mandolin, fiddle, and ukelin).

Philo Records, Dept. MB, The Barn, North Ferrisburg, VT 05743

Folk artists like Bodie Wagner, Utah Phillips, and Mary McCaslin (who also has albums on other labels, like Flying Fish), and various other choices like Boys of the Lough.

Rollin' Rock Records, Dept. MB, 6918 Peach Ave., Van Nuys, CA 91406

Good, clean rockabilly fun music. Many artists. The Magnetics are my big-time favorites. If you don't dance to this, you must be paralyzed!

Rounder Records, Dept. MB, 186 Willow Ave., Somerville, MA 02144

The Rounder catalog runs the full gamut of folk music from blues and country through ethnic, topical, and even rock-and-roll and jazz and has a huge selection, since this company distributes many other labels. A recent enormous success was a recording by George Thorogood and the Destroyers, a three-man blues-rock band, that sold into six figures—unheard of for an independent label up to then.

Roundup Records, Dept. MB, Box 147, East Cambridge, MA 02141

A mail-order distributor for many labels. All types of folk music. A catalog with a regular update newsletter is available.

Sanskrit Records, Dept. MB, 7515 Wayzata Blvd., No. 110, Minneapolis, MN 55426

Midwestern contemporary folk music.

Satyam Records, Dept. MB, P.O. Box 7 D.T.S., Canton, OH 44701

Guitar instrumentals to use with meditation.

Margaret Steinbuch, Dept. MB, 3572 Schwartz Ave., Cincinnati, OH 45211

Old standards on the musical saw by a charming grandmother who started her career in vaudeville, playing the violin!

Swallowtail Records, Dept. MB, Box 843, Ithaca, NY 14850

Traditional folk music, string bands, contemporary music.

Takoma Records, Dept. MB, P.O. Box 5369, Santa Monica, CA 90405

Started on the strength of John Fahey's solo guitar instrumental albums, and those of his protege, Leo Kottke, the label has branched out to include some fine live bluegrass albums, recorded at the concert hall next door (McCabe's Guitar Shop, Santa Monica). Various other choices are also available.

Train on the Island Records, Dept. MB, P.O. Box 9701, Minneapolis, MN 55440

A co-op record company (and co-op for booking musicians) with contemporary folk musicians from the Midwest.

Virgin Vinyl Records, Dept. MB, P.O. Box 92, Bothell, WA 98011

Rock and pop by Jef Jaisun, "the world's most obscure rock star." Novelty tunes like "I Smell Like 90 Weight" and "Friendly Neighborhood Narco Agent," as well as political folk-blues.

Voyager Recordings, Dept. MB, 424 35th Ave., Seattle, WA 98122

Old-time fiddling is a specialty here, but string bands, bluegrass, traditional jazz, contemporary African rhythm, and even classical sounds are also available. Dudley Hill's flat-picking guitar album and Rag Daddy's jug-band jazz are my favorites.

Wise Women Enterprises, Dept. MB, P.O. Box 297, West Station, NY 10014

Recordings by women artists only.

Yazoo Records, Dept. MB, 245 Waverly Place, New York, NY 10014

Blues—with a smattering of Hawaiian, jazz, and ragtime music—is the specialty here. Many recordings are reissues of classic bluesmen like Rev. Gary Davis, Big Bill Broonzy, and Blind Willie McTell.

CONSTRUCTION AND REPAIR MANUALS, AND OTHER BOOKS

You say the bridge just popped off your guitar? Or maybe the instrument has a crack in the back that you've been meaning to get fixed, but there's not a qualified repair person in the neighborhood. Relax. The guitar has grown so popular that a whole library of literature on its care and repair has sprung up. And if you're a serious guitar picker or collector, or if you're thinking of making some money by starting a musical-instrument repair business, you'll want to own at least a couple of the better manuals.

The following list contains nearly all of the available guitar-repair manuals, and all of the instrument-construction manuals I know about, as well as various other books related to homegrown music. Most of the books in this section are available from the bigger mail-order suppliers in the mail-order section. I list them here to help you become aware of what's available. You will find additional books listed in the mail-order catalogs.

The Acoustic Guitar: Adjustment, Care, Maintenance, and Repair, by Don E. Teeter, University of Oklahoma Press, Dept. MB, 1005 Asp Ave., Norman, OK 73019. 200 pages, hardbound.

Don Teeter was a guitar-playing machinist before he went into business repairing guitars. I suspect this practical background helps him write in plain language and provide simple but detailed explanations. *The Acoustic Guitar* is primarily for people who make a living fixing guitars (or would like to). It provides complete details of the design and construction of special repair tools, including some developed by Teeter himself. Furthermore, the book tells you how to use this equipment and discover techniques for working more efficiently with standard workshop tools.

Teeter's book receives my highest recommendation, and anyone serious enough to buy it should probably also obtain *Complete Guitar Repair*, by Hideo Kamimoto (see below), if not all of the repair manuals in this section.

The only specific "axe" not covered in *The Acoustic Guitar* is the arch-top, or plectrum, guitar. Happily, it's covered in *Complete Guitar Repair.* (Teeter has also released a sequel, with the same publisher.)

Classic Guitar Construction, by Irving Sloane, E.P. Dutton, Dept. MB, 201 Park Ave. S., New York, NY 10003.

Complete Banjo Repair, by Larry Sandburg, Oak Publications, Dept. MB, P.O. Box 572, 5 Bellevale Road, Tester, NY 10918.

Oak Publications is the largest publisher of all types of folk music instruction books in
Complete Guitar Repair, by Hideo Kamimoto, Oak Publications, Dept. MB, P.O. Box 572, 5 Bellevale Road, Tester, NY 10918. 160 pages, paperback. $6.95.
enthusiast. It pays a lot of attention to the special problems of the bluegrass instrument's unique hardware, woodwork and tone. Even though Sandburg's book deals only with five-string banjos, it is applicable to other varieties as well, since most repairs are made in the same way, regardless of the number of strings.

Now we need a banjo book equivalent to Wheeler's *Guitar Book* (see below).

Complete Guitar Repair, by Hideo Kamimoto, Oak Publications, Dept. MB, P.O. Box 572, 5 Bellevale Road, Tester, NY 10918. 160 pages, paperback. $6.95.

Mr. Kamimoto covers the basic designs of, and particular repair problems for, all of the different kinds of guitars from classic and flamenco through folk and flat-top, including both arch-top and solid-body electric instruments. He does assume that his readers have some knowledge of the subject, however, and the tone of the work is rather intellectual, especially when compared to Teeter's down-home style in *The Acoustic Guitar* (see above).

Complete Guitar Repair's section on equal tempered tuning in the repair shop is particularly interesting and provides in-depth information not offered anywhere else. In addition, there's a table of fret spacing calculations for guitars with scale lengths from 23½ inches to 26½ inches (in ⅛-inch intervals) and for electric basses with scale lengths from 30½ inches to 34½ inches (in ¼-inch intervals). You'll also find the usual chapter on each of the common repair jobs, such as warped necks (yes, Virginia, there is such a device as a neck straightener!), broken peg heads, fingerboard replacements, bridges, cracks and patches, touch-ups, and refinishing. The electric guitar is also discussed, in a section that includes the electronic aspects of the instrument as well as its mechanical functions.

I recommend that you make this book and Teeter's volume part of your repair-shop library. Certain techniques (such as refretting) are described differently in each book. That difference gives you a chance to choose the method that suits you best.

The Dobro Book, by Stacy Phillips, Oak Publications, Dept. MB, P.O. Box 572, 5 Bellevale Road, Tester, NY 10918.

Elderly Instruments Catalog, Elderly Instruments, Dept. MB, 541 E. Grand River, East Lansing, MI 48823.

More than a third of this catalog lists books, with descriptions of the contents in many cases. I can't recommend these people too highly. They're tops. They probably have all the books listed here in this section, and at discount prices too.

The Electric Guitar: Its History and Construction, by Donald Brosnac, Panjandrum Books, Dept. MB, 99 Sanchez St., San Francisco, CA 94114. 96 pages, paperback. $5.95.

Here again we have two sets of blueprints for electric guitars: A Fender Stratocaster-style solid body and a thin-line double-cutaway hollow body, both drawn at one-half scale.

This volume is a little shorter than *The Steel String Guitar*, Brosnac's other book (see below), but the construction of an electric guitar is simpler than that of the acoustic variety. The details of making the instruments are presented in outline form rather than as a complete description. All of the steps are listed, but particular problems and techniques in woodworking are not specifically covered. However, electric pickup design is described in enough detail to allow most folks to build their own.

Fix Your Axe, compiled by the editors of Guitar Player Books, Dept. MB, P.O. Box 615, Saratoga, CA 95070, 72 pages, paperback. $5.95.

The cover says it all: It's a picture of some poor fellow leaning out of his car window to discover that he's just run over his guitar case. You can bet *that* repair job isn't covered in this book!

One theme that's stressed in *Fix Your Axe* is that some repairs are better left in professional hands, and I agree, if you're tempted to try such work while relying only on the sketchy information presented in this volume. It's true that you can create a more serious repair job from a lesser one through error, but such a disaster isn't likely to happen if you can also refer to the clearer and more thorough instructions presented in *The Acoustic Guitar* and *Complete Guitar Repair* (see above).

The Guitar Book, by Tom Wheeler, Harper and Row, Dept. MB, 10 East 53rd St., New York, NY 10022. 343 pages, hardbound. $18.

More than just a book, this work is a monument to the guitar. I feel that the chapters about adjustment and repair are too short, but they're not the reasons why I recommend this volume anyway. I was more impressed by the fascinating information about the guitar: Its origin and history, photographs of rare and significant models, portraits of famous players, chapters on how to choose a guitar and strings, a hearty section on amplifiers and speakers, special effects, and so forth.

Over half of the book is devoted to electric guitars and related technology, so it's not for those of you who aren't into electronics. But I can wholeheartedly recommend that everyone else go buy it, or pester your local library to purchase it. It's worth the somewhat steep price.

Guitar Repair, by Irving Sloane, E.P. Dutton, Dept. MB, 201 Park Ave. S., New York, NY 10003. 95 pages, hardbound. $8.95.

The primary appeal of *Guitar Repair* is the excellent photography of repair work being done at the Martin Guitar Factory in Nazareth, Pennsylvania.

Hammered Dulcimer, by Peter Pickow, Oak Publications, Dept. MB, 33 W. 60th St., New York, NY 10023.

Home Recording for the Musician, by Craig Anderton, Guitar Player Books, Dept. MB, P.O. Box 615, Saratoga, CA 95070.

How to Make and Sell Your Own Record, by Diane Sward Rapaport, Headlands Press, Dept. MB, P.O. Box 862, Tiburon, CA 94920.

Illustrated Encyclopedia of Country Music, by Roy Thompson and Fred Deller, Harmony Books, Dept. MB, One Park Ave., New York, NY 10016.

International Guide to Music Festivals, by Douglas Smith and Nancy Barton, Quick Fox, Dept MB, 33 W. 60th St., New York, NY 10023.

Jean Ritchie's Dulcimer People, by Jean Ritchie, Oak Publications, Dept. MB, P.O. Box 572, 5 Bellevale Road, Tester, NY 10918.

This one has a section on building your own dulcimer by Hank Levin, who is one of the kit suppliers listed in the mail-order section of *Resources*.

Making Musical Instruments, by Irving Sloane, E.P. Dutton, Dept. MB, 201 Park Ave. S., New York, NY 10003.

Piano Tuning, by J. Cree Fischer, Dover Publications, Inc., Dept. MB, 180 Varick St., New York, NY 10014.

Is the old family heirloom a bit out of tune? Even *more* than a bit? Although hiring a piano tuner isn't really as expensive as you might imagine, you still can't beat the cost of doing it yourself or the satisfaction of completing an intricate job with your own two hands.

Although Fischer's book was first published way back in 1907, it's still chock full of timely information on the proper way to tune a piano, whether the instrument is an upright, a square, or a grand. The volume is subtitled *A Simple and Accurate Method for Amateurs*, and that's exactly what it is. Using plain English, the author teaches you the easiest technique for "setting the temper" of your piano. You'll even learn how to remove and repair the entire action (or key and hammer works) of a standard instrument, and that skill—who knows?—could lead to a profitable home business in restoring old, worn-out keyboard music-makers.

Steel String Guitar Construction, by Irving Sloane, E.P. Dutton, Dept. MB, 201 Park Ave. S., New York, NY 10003.

A "Homegrown Music" reader recommends this one.

The Steel String Guitar: Construction and Repair, by David Russell Young, Chilton Book Co., Dept. MB, 201 King of Prussia Rd., Radnor, PA 19089. 158 pages, hardbound. $12.50.

There's only one set of plans in this manual, and the section on repairs is even shorter than is the equivalent chapter in *The Guitar Book*, but Young's volume contains comprehensive instructions on how to build a guitar.

Young, like Donald Brosnac, advocates an unorthodox method of attaching the instrument's neck to its body. He just flat glues it on with epoxy! This is simpler than most other methods, to be sure, and permanent as hell, so be certain your work is right the first time! The author also uses a nonadjustable reinforcing rod in the neck, making the matter of setting action for different string gauges difficult. He recommends matching the gauge to the guitar as is (and if that doesn't work, you'll have to replace the fret board to get the sound you want).

Such design idiosyncracies do amount to simplifications for the person who is just starting to build or repair guitars, and the descriptions of each step (including, in some cases, the building of jigs and forms) are fairly complete and well illustrated. This is a well-written book, beautifully designed and illustrated, and I recommend it to anyone who aspires to build steel string guitars. (See also *Guild of American Luthiers Quarterly*, in the folk music publications section.)

The Steel String Guitar: Its Construction, Origin and Design, by Donald Brosnac, Panjandrum Books, Dept. MB, 99 Sanchez St., San Francisco, CA 94114. 112 pages, paperback. $5.95.

Although it's hardly complete in the treatment of its subject, this book may be of use to some of you because it contains blueprints and instructions for building two different styles of acoustic steel string guitars. Both the Gibson B-25 and the standard dreadnought model are presented in blueprint form (one-half scale). Brosnac favors the Spanish-style neck joint (with a slotted integral headblock), which is somewhat unorthodox but completely serviceable. He treats the standard dovetail joint, briefly, at the end of the construction section.

Of course, questions will come up while you are making your instrument—even if you have some experience and skill in woodworking—and many of those questions won't be answered in this, or any, book. Actually, if you're going to construct a guitar, you'll learn as much from simply doing it as you will from reading about the subject, and probably a lot more.

To get started, you just need a basic design, a list of tools and materials, and an outline of the steps of construction. *The Steel String Guitar* provides these essentials, though the steps are not as detailed as you might like.